A SPY CALLED CYNTHIA

A SPY CALLED CYNTHIA
AND A LIFE IN INTELLIGENCE

ANONYMOUS

Biteback Publishing

First published in Great Britain in 2021 by
Biteback Publishing Ltd, London
Copyright © Anonymous 2021

ISBN 978-1-78590-712-8

10 9 8 7 6 5 4 3 2 1

A CIP catalogue record for this book is available from the British Library.

Set in Adobe Caslon Pro and Din

Printed and bound in Great Britain by
CPI Group (UK) Ltd, Croydon CR0 4YY

I was her controller, but it wasn't long before I started to wonder who was controlling who.

FOREWORD

This is the story of a British spymaster's relationship with one of the most important female intelligence agents in the Second World War, of his involvement in the subsequent fiasco of Kim Philby and the Cambridge spies and his friendships with counterparts in the CIA and the remarkable Count Alexandre de Marenches in France.

You may feel that it should belong on the fiction shelves of your bookshop or library because, although virtually all of it undoubtedly did happen and is part of the historical record, I cannot guarantee its entire authenticity. Cynthia's family were adamant that she did not have an affair with the author, who was for a while her intelligence controller, and who can say if they were not right. Perhaps he just imagined that aspect of this story – or made it up. I must leave it to the reader to form his or her own view. They also contended that the havoc she wreaked amidst the Italian and Vichy French embassy staffs owed more to her sparkling conversation than to her undoubted physical attractions; a theory I would have to take with a very large grain of salt.

But, if I cannot vouch for the personal aspects of this story, I can guarantee the accuracy of this account of the exploits of Cynthia as a secret agent of British intelligence in the War.

I too worked for the government, in close cooperation with the security agencies. This manuscript was given me by my far more senior colleague, who was a friend and mentor to me. It was not, he said, to be published 'until everyone in it is dead, including me!' As that has long since been the case, I have arranged for it to be published now, as I promised him I would.

I have made some amendments, for purposes of clarification and the avoidance of jargon, and interspersed some subheadings. Nowhere have I changed the sense of what he wrote.

Robin Renwick, former British ambassador to the United States

THE ALIBI CLUB

The snow was still on the ground in Washington DC on the February evening when I presented myself, as instructed, at the door of the Alibi Club, a small brownstone building in the capital. Membership was limited to fifty. I had been made an honorary member during my service there during the War. Another honorary member was said to be the Shah of Persia, though I never saw him there. He was proposed by Kim Roosevelt, who, by engineering the overthrow of the Prime Minister Mosaddegh, who was bent on nationalising the Western oil companies in Persia, had helped to make him the real ruler of his country.

During the War, the Club had been taken over by senior members of the Office of Strategic Services (OSS), the wartime precursor of the CIA. They had included Colonel 'Wild Bill' Donovan, head of the OSS, and still did include Ambassador David Bruce, Richard Helms and other intelligence veterans of the War. The staff bore an uncanny resemblance to one another, all being rather venerable, grey-haired, dignified black Washingtonians, all of whom had been subject to security vetting by the Agency. They were not supposed ever to disclose what was discussed within the confines of the Club and, as far as I know, none of them ever did.

The Club's name was based on the notion that if any lady rang up to enquire about the whereabouts of her husband, she would be told that he was within its doors, but could not be disturbed, whatever his whereabouts; a stratagem very rarely employed, and unlikely to fool anybody. The upstairs sitting room was full of memorabilia from exotic locations, with one or two African masks, plus numerous postcards of scantily clad ladies in Paris, Tangier and Istanbul.

Mr Allen Dulles, I was told, was running a bit late, but would be there shortly. And sure enough, soon I heard his booming voice, announcing his arrival and bursting into the dining room, followed by his cohort from the CIA. Prominent among them was Richard Bissell, Dulles's current favourite, who had developed the U-2 spy plane programme, but who was to bring down himself and his boss through his mad adventure in the Bay of Pigs. I had of course heard the stories of some anti-Castro exiles being given military training in Central America. But I did not imagine that the Agency would be so foolhardy as to land a few hundred of them, with no air cover, on swampy ground on the Cuban coast, in the expectation that this would trigger a general uprising, of which, in the event, there was no sign whatever.

Neither Dulles nor Bissell would ever have dared to propose such a hare-brained scheme to Eisenhower, but they had somehow persuaded the new President and his brother, Bobby, to let them try. It transpired that Bissell's calculation had been that once the exiles were attacked, as they were, by Castro's rickety aircraft, the President would order the US Air Force to intervene, which he declined to do.

But this was before that fiasco. Dulles still was in his pomp. He had not yet been deflated. Helms, who turned out to have opposed the entire scheme, barely spoke for the entire evening.

Having obliged us all to drink large martinis consisting, so far as I could taste, of straight gin, an olive and no vermouth, Dulles installed us at the large round table and announced that they were about to hear the story of the most important female agent in the Second World War and, in his judgement, one of the most valuable of all the agents we had ever had at our disposal.

I smiled inwardly at this, for there was never any question of according Cynthia precedence over Dulles's favourite agent, Admiral Canaris, head of Hitler's intelligence agency, the *Abwehr*, whom Dulles never met, but who had started sending messages to him in Switzerland at a late stage, once he had become convinced that Germany was bound to lose the War.

I was never entirely convinced that Canaris was really an agent at all. He was trying to hedge his bets and to ensure that as much of Germany as possible ended up under the Western powers and not under the Russians. But maybe I was mistaken, for he was disloyal enough to get himself executed on Hitler's orders in the final weeks of the War. Dulles's well-publicised liaison with Canaris had helped to propel him to the top of the CIA.

I was not, I was sure, alone in feeling that there was a ghost at this dinner – that of Frank Wisner, the Agency's head of covert operations, who had been the ebullient life and soul of many similar gatherings. The can-do, hyperactive Wisner had landed successive teams of exiles in Albania, only for nearly all of them to be rounded up and shot thanks, as he later discovered, to the treachery of Kim Philby. But the nadir for Frank had come with the Hungarian uprising that was ruthlessly suppressed by Soviet tanks in 1956. Frank rushed to the Austria/Hungary border, traumatised by the fact that he felt that the Hungarians had been encouraged to revolt by Radio Free Europe, which the Agency had founded and funded, only for them then to find that there was nothing the US could or would do to help them. Frank never really recovered from this debacle. He had to be invalided out of the Agency (and, after a long period of depression, committed suicide).

Most of those present already knew something of the story of Cynthia and how close I had been to her. As I ran through her extraordinary achievements, omitting the personal elements, the whole story flashed at an accelerated pace through my brain.

But first I had better explain how it was that, by accident, I ended up in the shadowy world of intelligence and became Cynthia's controller, though it was not long before I started to wonder who was controlling who.

NARVIK AND TRONDHEIM

On Sunday 3 September 1939, I and the other senior members of Rowe & Pitman had heard on a crackling radio the Prime Minister, Neville Chamberlain, announcing in a quavering voice that as Hitler had invaded Poland, which we had undertaken with the French to protect, we were now at war with Germany.

On the following afternoon, some of the younger members of the firm and I walked up the road to the headquarters of the Honourable Artillery Company in the City to see if we could enlist in the Army. It took an hour before I was summoned into the presence of a sergeant who, on taking down my particulars, said that, as I was thirty, my services would not be required any time soon, if – he implied – at all. There might be some sort of reserve role for me at home, depending on the requirements later.

I trudged back to the office well aware that, although

I had tried, this news would not go down well with my wife Caroline's very military family. For her father was a tough and weather-beaten retired Admiral, who had commanded a cruiser in the Battle of Jutland and felt that his daughter had married beneath her. I thought vaguely of the tales of women in the First World War presenting white feathers to men apparently of military age still in civilian clothes.

So when, on returning to Oxford, I explained this fiasco to my wife, I asked her to arrange a meeting with the old sea dog, her father, in case he could find a way to help to get me into the Navy. The response from the Admiral was an invitation to lunch at his favourite watering hole, the Army and Navy Club in Pall Mall.

He proved surprisingly helpful. One of his former colleagues, he said, had been drafted into the Admiralty in some kind of staff job. He would ask if he could think of anything for me.

There followed a further invitation to lunch at the Army and Navy Club, this time from the colleague he had described as Godfrey, which I thought must be his first name. In fact this turned out to be Rear Admiral John Godfrey, whose idea of lunch was decidedly Spartan (no wine).

Why was I so keen to join the Navy, he enquired. Because I had been turned down by the Army, I replied. Realising that this was not the right response, I added that

I could not see myself just going on selling shares and bonds when there was a war on.

This showed the right spirit, in Godfrey's view. He seemed mildly interested in the fact that I had a law degree, which might come in handy, he thought. I would be hearing from him.

Ten days later I received a letter from the Admiralty instructing me to procure two copies of the uniform of a temporary lieutenant in the Royal Naval Volunteer Reserve from the naval outfitters in Piccadilly. I was then to present myself to the Royal Naval College in Dartmouth for basic training.

Our training consisted of the endless repetition of naval drills, plus more interesting visits to have explained to us the equipment and *modus operandi* of a destroyer and a frigate in the harbour. We learned every detail of Nelson's suicidal tactics in the Battle of Trafalgar, plus the fact that the French admiral, Villeneuve, had tried to persuade Napoleon that, despite having – with the Spanish – more ships, he should not go out to fight, as Nelson was not a normal adversary and would destroy them all.

I asked if it might not make more sense for us to study the Battle of Jutland, of which I had heard many accounts from my father-in-law. As the Germans had inflicted more damage on our ships than we had on theirs, how could we regard this as a victory? The instructor patiently replied that it was indeed a victory as the German fleet had never again ventured out into the North Sea until their great ships were escorted to Scapa Flow to be scuttled after the German surrender.

After eight weeks in Dartmouth I was told to report to the Admiralty in Whitehall. There I was escorted to the domain of Admiral Godfrey in Room 39, which was in fact a series of inter-connecting rooms, presided over by Ian Fleming, who had established himself as the Admiral's personal assistant. I knew Ian from his not very successful stock-broking days. I had found him hard to like, as he had private means, could afford to live more grandly than me and appeared to look down on those of us who couldn't. His Bentley was a decided step up on my MG. But during the War, he was an effective assistant to Godfrey and, as for his much later success as an author, I devoured his novels as enthusiastically as John F. Kennedy loved to do.

I was assigned to the Scandinavian desk, where the main issue was the fact that the Swedes were shipping vast quantities of iron ore to feed the German military machine. Our disgusted naval attaché in Stockholm had to be withdrawn for declaring that 'the Swedish flag is blue, but has a yellow streak in it'. A covert attempt by us at sabotage had achieved nothing, other than to infuriate the Swedes.

Knowing nothing whatever about Scandinavia, I made little progress but in the New Year I had the good fortune to befriend the Norwegian naval attaché, Uwe Johannson, a huge sailor with a vast amount of facial hair. Two formal calls were followed by an invitation to meet him in a nightclub in Soho, where I found him accompanied by a Women's Royal Navy (Wren) cadet about half his size. To make up the numbers, I invited Godfrey's PA, who was quite attractive and had been helping me to find my way around the Admiralty.

After dancing with the Wren firmly attached to his chest, her feet barely touching the ground, Uwe ordered a bottle of Scotch and turned his attention to me. Did we not realise, he said, that Hitler was bound to attack Norway as soon as the ice melted within a few weeks? The reason was obvious. Without controlling Norwegian waters the Germans would be unable to get their warships out into and beyond the North Sea.

If we waited for the Germans to invade it would be too late. We absolutely must occupy the Norwegian ports of Narvik and Trondheim before the Germans did. The Swedes were shipping much of their iron ore through Narvik. His government were clinging to their neutrality, but that had no chance of saving them.

These trips to the unpretentious nightclub in Greek Street became regular outings for the four of us. By this time I was engaged in a mild affair with Godfrey's friendly PA. Neither of us took it too seriously and I departed back to my family at the weekend. Inevitably, it transpired that Ian Fleming, of whom she did not have a high opinion, had preceded me in her affections. 'A bit of a cad,' was her opinion and that of some others too.

Uwe became increasingly insistent about the imperative need for us to seize the Norwegian ports. The ice would be melting and very soon it would be too late.

So pressing was he that, in early March, I summoned the courage to write a memo to Godfrey summarising his plan, though, at his insistence, I left Uwe's name out of it. Godfrey was sufficiently excited by this to send it up to the First Lord's office. Two days later it came back with a scribbled note from Churchill on it: 'An error – but very much in the right direction.' His private secretary said that, in reality, he agreed. But King Haakon of Norway was best friends with our King and we could not just trample all over him. Nonetheless, Churchill did press for the mining of Narvik waters, which was resisted by Chamberlain until that too was too late.

On 9 April, the Germans launched their blitzkrieg into Denmark and Norway. The ensuing campaign went exactly as Uwe had predicted. It was the very model of how not to wage a war. We rushed ships and men across to the Norwegian ports, but not in sufficient time or numbers to stop the Germans, who had seized all the near impregnable strategic positions in and around the fjords we should have seized before them. Our ships were bombarded by well-positioned land-based artillery. By early June, we had to withdraw. The only benefit from this fiasco was Churchill displacing Chamberlain as Prime Minister.

This episode earned me a rare compliment from the

Admiral: 'We should bloody well have done what you advised.'

WILLIAM STEPHENSON

Several weeks later, I was told to report to Major General Stewart Menzies, head of the Secret Intelligence Service (SIS). Godfrey told me that Menzies had heard about the Trondheim and Narvik memo. I walked the short distance from the Admiralty to the SIS headquarters in Broadway wondering what this summons was all about.

Menzies, an Old Etonian who had served with distinction in the Life Guards in the First World War, received me rather stiffly. Was I available to go abroad at short notice? He explained that the new Prime Minister had appointed a Canadian wartime friend of his to head our operations against the Germans in the United States. William Stephenson was a splendid chap – a former fighter pilot – who had 'dabbled' in intelligence on his own account, said Menzies rather disapprovingly. It was in fact Stephenson who had got us into 'a spot of bother' in Sweden, with his plans to sabotage the iron ore supplies. He needed me to join his operation in New York to ensure a close relationship with and some guidance from the SIS headquarters in Broadway.

Having always wanted to go to America, I accepted

forthwith. As I walked back across the park, I realised that I had just been given my first intelligence assignment – which was to report to Stewart Menzies on the activities of William Stephenson.

Menzies, I was later to discover, was more of a Whitehall warrior than a great spymaster himself, as Stephenson undoubtedly was, but an unrivalled operator vis-à-vis the government. His reputation with Churchill was based on the fact that it was Menzies who took him the most important intercepts from the 'Ultra' signals material produced by our cryptologists in their Nissen huts in Bletchley Park, though Menzies otherwise had no involvement there at all.

I made the tortuous journey to New York by air, refuelling in Reykjavik and Newfoundland. It was impossible not to be excited on arrival in this throbbing city, with no shortages and the lights on everywhere at night, which appeared to be and was oblivious to the War raging several thousand miles away.

I was installed in a comfortable hotel near the impressive offices of what described itself as the UK Passport Control Office, in fact British Security Coordination (BSC), on the thirty-sixth floor of the Rockefeller Plaza. Stephenson's welcome was far warmer than my somewhat chilly encounter with Menzies. He invariably would end the day with his favourite martini, often in our company. He did not say much but he demanded action, frequently of an unconventional kind, especially in countering the

German American *Bund*, which was active in insisting on US neutrality while seeking to harm us in every way they could.

I was taken by a colleague to a clandestine meeting with hard-boiled union officials in the port, who we were paying to help protect our shipping and inform us about that of the Germans. Before long they were engaged in some acts of sabotage on our account as well. Stephenson had established a cautious live and let live understanding with J. Edgar Hoover of the FBI because Hoover, on checking, had found that he had support from the Roosevelt White House, including from Robert Sherwood, who was far more than just a speechwriter to the President. Stephenson had been helped in making some very important contacts by his friend, the former heavyweight boxing champion, Gene Tunney. Hoover later sought and received confirmation that the President himself had met Stephenson.

One of Stephenson's closest friends was Nelson Rockefeller. Visiting Stephenson years later in his retirement in Bermuda, I mentioned that his friend, sadly, had expired in the arms of a much younger girlfriend.

'What a way to go!' was Stephenson's apparently approving comment.

I enjoyed the camaraderie of the Stephenson operation, and his assiduous cultivation of the US press, who in their vast majority were on our side. One of my favourite colleagues was David Ogilvy, who had playboy proclivities, but who later was to use his undoubted charm to become king of the advertising industry in the US.

Reminiscing after the War in his retirement in Bermuda, Stephenson was accused of embellishing his own legend (as most of us tend to do). The name by which he became known, 'Intrepid', was not his codename, but his telegraphic address, chosen for him by Stephenson himself. But it reflected the character of the man, and his legend was over 90 per cent true. For his achievements in the War far exceeded those of SIS elsewhere in the world. To have established a US-wide intelligence operation on the scale and with the influence that Stephenson succeeded in doing was as great an achievement as there ever has been in the world of intelligence. Overcoming the rivalries between them, BSC progressively incorporated the activities of SIS, MI5 and the Special Operations Executive (SOE) in North America, integrating them far more effectively than in the UK. And Stephenson managed to do so in the face of extreme continued wariness from Hoover and the outright hostility of influential US dignitaries like Adolf Berle, who kept urging his boss, Secretary of State Cordell Hull, to close down 'the British spy organisation in the United States'. Stephenson also played a crucial role in helping to persuade Roosevelt to agree to lend fifty American destroyers to us in August 1940.

By this time, however, my own role was being rather eclipsed, as Menzies appointed one of his deputies, Dick Ellis, to represent him in New York.

I was saved by Admiral Godfrey, who sent me a message to say that his man in Washington, one of the assistant naval attachés, was being promoted to command a frigate. I was to replace him and was being promoted to lieutenant commander 'to help the locals to take you seriously', Godfrey declared.

So I migrated to a small clapboard house in Georgetown, close to the heart of Washington in a neighbourhood inhabited by many members of the Roosevelt administration. Later, I moved to a suite in the Shoreham Hotel. My office was not in the embassy but in an annex off Dupont Circle, which was intended to be more discreet.

To my relief, I found myself in the hands of a highly competent secretary, who was married to one of the vice-consuls. She put me in touch with my predecessor's contacts in the US Navy. When I met his principal counterpart in the FBI, I got a frosty reception. 'Please tell your friends in New York,' he said, 'that they need to stay on the right side of the law.'

My very formal meeting with the ambassador, Lord Halifax, a well-known former appeaser despatched by Winston Churchill to Washington to get him out of the War Cabinet, confirmed the general impression of him as the worst kind of stuffed shirt. Shortly after arriving in Washington, he had got an appalling press by riding out with the Virginia hunt in a red tunic. But his staff were a lot more welcoming and invited me to a couple of embassy parties, at one of which I met a press contact who was to prove very useful to me.

'LOOKS LIKE A MAN-EATER TO ME'

My formidable secretary guided me through the files left behind by my predecessor. It did not take long to find a report from the MI6 representative in Warsaw, Colonel Jack Shelley, about the Washington debutante, the daughter of a distinguished Marine Corps veteran and of a well-known socialite, who had married a not very distinguished British diplomat, 'rather a dull dog', a lot older than her. When he fell seriously ill and had to return to London, she had remained in Warsaw where she had caused a scandal by having an affair with a Polish cavalry officer, who was an aide-de-camp to the Chief of Staff of the Polish Army.

For several months we and the French had been discussing with the Polish cryptographers ways of attacking the German military codes. We knew that they had acquired copies of the German Enigma machines. But it was Colonel Shelley's friend, and by now agent, Cynthia who, by cultivating a relationship with a member of the Polish Foreign Ministry, was first to confirm that the Poles finally had succeeded in decyphering some German Enigma traffic, which they had not yet confided to us.

This had led up to the meeting in Warsaw not long

before the German invasion, at which the Poles had handed over to us and the French one replica each of the German Enigma machines and explained to the doyen of our cryptographers, Dilly Knox, their methods in decrypting the German Enigma codes. Cynthia had assisted in the planning to get the Polish team out of Warsaw and the country in the event of a German invasion. (Colonel Shelley put them on the train from Warsaw to Brest-Litovsk, then on to Romania, from where they ended up in France only for the French, to our frustration, not to let any of them move on to Britain.)

Although her friend in the Foreign Ministry had advanced his cause by playing Chopin to her, Cynthia soon aimed higher by engaging in an affair with the head of the office of the Polish Foreign Minister, Colonel Józef Beck, which provided some very useful intelligence indeed for her reports had exposed Colonel Beck as playing a double game. While seeking guarantees of help from us and the French, he also had negotiated with Hitler for Poland to acquire a slice of Czech territory when the Germans occupied Czechoslovakia.

In her own reminiscences of Warsaw, she airbrushed out the cavalry officer but was justifiably proud of the amount of information she had extracted from the Foreign Minister's *chef de cabinet*, Michał Łubienski, who was later to feature in the Polish government in exile in London.

Their liaison became known to Colonel Beck, who

protested about it to the straight-laced British ambassador, causing him to insist that Cynthia must return forthwith to London, overruling the protests of Colonel Shelley, who was losing by far his best source, though by then it was not long before the embassy had to be evacuated anyway.

After a few months back with her husband, who had been posted to Santiago, she had left him and returned to her family's home in Virginia.

'Handle with care,' was the advice. But she detested the Germans and had told Shelley that she would be willing to help in any way she could.

* * *

It took me longer than it should have done to work out just how Cynthia could be engaged. But gradually a plan started to crystallise in my mind. My colleagues from BSC in New York contacted her mother, a well-known figure in Washington and Virginia, to suggest that her daughter should call in to see me.

When I returned from lunch a few days later, my secretary said, with the hint of a smirk, 'She's waiting in your office.' There wasn't anywhere else for her to wait and clearly she had been studying Cynthia's file.

As I walked into the room, I encountered the faint scent of an expensive perfume. Cynthia stood up, smoothing down imaginary wrinkles in her impeccable skirt, to greet me with a firm handshake and a warm smile.

She was wearing a cream silk shirt and smart jacket with a skirt shorter than what passed for normal at the time, barely covering her knees and not covering them at all when she crossed her attractive legs, as she proceeded from time to time to do. Careful make-up – not too much – blonde-ish hair and wide-set eyes completed an extremely attractive picture.

I discovered later that her role model was the movie actress Carole Lombard. She dressed like her, dyed her hair blonde-ish and generally tried to look like her, helped by the fact that there was a resemblance anyway.

She was very nervous. Did I mind if she smoked? Of course not. I leaned forward with a lighter as, with a slightly trembling hand, she placed a cigarette between her lips.

'What have they been telling you about me?' she enquired.

'That you might be prepared to help us again, as you did in Poland,' I replied. 'You got a good report from Colonel Shelley,' I added.

'Oh, but I *loved* the Colonel!' was her theatrical response. 'I didn't speak any Polish and I had nothing to do, except go to embassy parties,' she declared. 'I was thrilled to be asked to help him.'

She seemed to be well suited to what I had in mind.

But I needed a bit of time to reflect. 'I think we might have something for you,' I said.

'That would be wonderful,' was the reply. 'I hate the Germans. You will have heard about their Stukas machine-gunning refugees in Poland. If you do, I'll give it my best shot.'

No longer nervous, she was now glowing with excitement. She looked ready to throw her arms around my neck. Instead I gave her a rather stiff handshake.

'What did you think?' I asked my secretary.

'Looks like a man-eater to me,' was the reply.

*   *   *

A few days later, at my request, she was back.

I explained that a key task assigned to me was to target the German, Italian and Vichy French embassies, all still in Washington at this stage of the War, by whatever means we could. I wanted her to help with this. The deputy editor of the local glossy magazine, precursor of the *Washingtonian*, was of British origin. She would agree to employ Cynthia – paid for by us – to cover their national days and other events for the journal. Given her attractive appearance, it should not be difficult for her to get to know some of their officials well.

Cynthia was thrilled but also, this time, very business-like. We would, I said, rent a small house for her in Georgetown and give her an allowance so that she could entertain any persons of interest to us. We would need to find unobtrusive venues for us to meet. How did she feel about this assignment?

'Leave it to me,' was her confident reply.

Wanting to understand her better, over lunch in a quiet corner of Chevy Chase, I asked what had happened in her marriage. It had all been a terrible mistake was the short answer. It will sound to you like a bad dime novel, she added.

She had been invited by her mother to travel to Europe, which they had done on the *Queen Mary*. Invited to the Captain's table, she had encountered Arthur Pack, who was twenty years older and far worldlier than her. He was a commercial attaché in the British embassy who she had met briefly in Washington. On the ship, he had seemed important and looked impressive in his white dinner jacket.

She and her mother went on to Paris and Rome, then back to Washington where she caught up with Arthur Pack. Her socially ambitious mother thought that he was a suitable match. They had to get married in a hurry as she found that she was pregnant.

'My mistake', she said, 'was being just twenty years old. I had graduated *cum laude* from college but, in reality, I knew nothing about anything.' She added that she had also been determined to get away from her domineering mother.

She soon discovered that she barely knew the person

she had married. They spent a few months in Spain in the early days of the Civil War. She found it all exciting, but Arthur didn't find anything exciting and nor did he seem very interested in her. He seemed older than his years, due to illness, extremely fussy and not much fun to be with. They had turned out to have nothing in common at all.

I learned later that Arthur Pack had been so concerned about the scandal that would ensue if she produced a child in Washington so soon after their marriage that he insisted that it must be born in Britain and handed over to foster parents there. Though Cynthia never displayed any maternal instincts at all and barely visited the child in the ensuing years, this episode must have helped to undermine whatever bond she had formed with the person she had married.

She told me subsequently that in Spain the embassy had been evacuated to Biarritz but she had crossed back into Spain several times to take medical supplies and to rescue her 'first real love', a Spanish Air Force pilot who was being held by the Republicans in Valencia, while her husband had remained in Biarritz.

To be fair to him, it must have been well-nigh impossible to cope with Cynthia's extreme restlessness and recklessness and he had helped to evacuate the embassy staff to Biarritz. He was not a negligible figure. In 1918 he had served as a machine-gun instructor to American GIs arriving in France. He may, understandably, have longed for a less stressful partner than Cynthia. Although no star of the foreign service, he was regarded as a very competent commercial counsellor in his later posts in Latin America.

When they were posted to Warsaw, she told me, she found herself knowing hardly anyone, not understanding a word of Polish and with nothing to do until, thank goodness, Colonel Shelley asked her to help with his Polish contacts. When her husband suffered a stroke and was invalided back to London she had stayed on to work for the Colonel. Arthur, of course, had been furious about the embarrassment with the Polish officer, but in Biarritz he had turned out to have a girlfriend of his own. The marriage was already on the rocks when he was transferred to Santiago and she ended up leaving him to his own devices there.

'Have I passed your interrogation?' she enquired.

I said that anyone who proved uninterested in her seemed incomprehensible to me.

*   *   *

A few weeks later, I invited her to lunch again at a tiny inn in the countryside, west of Washington. Cynthia, this time, had produced a written report. The German embassy, predictably, was proving the most difficult target. Two of their diplomats had invited her out. But they never stopped boasting about all the Führer's victories. There was not the slightest hint of dissidence.

The French were very friendly, deluging her with

invitations. But by a strange chance, the Italian naval attaché, now an Admiral, was someone she had known socially when he had been an attaché in Washington in her debutante days. He was now married with two children, but it was clear that he was going to be her main target.

Two weeks later we met again, on our own, but in the house of her colleague on the magazine. I warned her that her friend, Admiral Alberto Lais, had been the head of naval intelligence in Italy. Part of his job was to report on our shipping to and from the United States, using members of the Italian-American community to help him in doing so. What, if anything, had he divulged?

Cynthia said that the Admiral took himself very seriously. When she had known him in her teens he had matinee idol looks and still was very vain. She had taunted him by pointing out that the Italian Navy had remained in port since the beginning of the War, even though the British had launched an air attack on their base at Taranto. Did they intend to keep this up until it ended?

The Admiral, very wounded, had said certainly not. There was no question of the fleet remaining in port for the duration of the War. That would be dishonourable. Its mission was to win control of the eastern Mediterranean and before long she would see it taking action to do so.

I thought this might be pie in the sky, but I reported it to London, where it was received with interest as, they said, there had been one or two similar indications from other sources.

The Admiral by now was besotted with her, according to Cynthia. He suspected that she might be working for US intelligence, certainly not the British. He was talking of divorce and of settling down with her in the US after the War. What was the most valuable information she could extract from him?

I replied that the crown jewels London were looking for were the Italian naval codes. But I had no idea how we could get hold of them. Cynthia didn't seem to either, but was looking very thoughtful.

One month later, in the course of a routine liaison meeting with him, my main contact in the FBI suddenly observed that 'your agent' had got extremely close to the Italian naval attaché, who of course was under observation by the Bureau. Was I sure that she was not herself a security risk?

I said that we had full confidence in her. Well, said my friend, she is now shacked up with the Admiral. They had been spending nights together at the Willard Hotel. So long as the flow of information was from the Admiral to us, and not the other way round, that was fine with him. But I would need to make sure of that.

I managed not to display any emotion. But inside I was feeling very emotional indeed. A knot had formed in my stomach that would not go away. I had been careful to keep my relations with Cynthia strictly correct as it was absolutely taboo for one of Godfrey's Naval Intelligence officers to become involved with one of his agents (she was in fact my only one, apart from a couple of friendly journalists) and I had no intention of doing so. But I had not been immune to Cynthia's attractiveness and special brand of animal magnetism. Was I jealous of the Admiral? The answer was furiously so. I was also furious with her.

'YOU DIDN'T BELIEVE THAT I COULD DO IT, DID YOU?'

At our next meeting, she told me that she had not yet broached the subject with him, but she thought there was a good chance she could inveigle the cyphers out of her paramour.

The Admiral was twice her age and she claimed that their relationship was 'mainly sentimental', which I doubted. But 'He is mad about me,' she declared cheerfully. She had started to tell him that she needed something to show her American friends that he really could be counted on, if he genuinely wished to settle with her in the US after the War.

I was sure he was besotted with her, but I made the mistake of saying that I could not believe that any naval officer would give away his country's cyphers. This produced a fiery reaction.

'Well, you are quite a stuffed shirt, aren't you?' she observed. 'I don't suppose that you have ever been madly in love with anyone, have you?'

I had to admit to myself that this was true. Backtracking hastily, I said that London would be for ever grateful if she could get hold of the cyphers, which could make a vital difference in the naval war.

She left with a snort and, as she told me afterwards, with an absolute determination to show me what she was capable of.

*   *   *

The Admiral spent much of the next few weeks in Cynthia's arms, with occasional bursts of weeping – from her lover, not from her. For, with Mussolini increasingly resentful of Roosevelt's support for the British, he knew that his time in the United States was drawing to a close. He was told by Cynthia that unless he proved his *bona fides* with the cyphers, it would be impossible for him to return to the United States or for them to see each other again after the War. He had told her that the cypher books were about to be replaced, so what would be the harm in this?

As I had expected, the Admiral balked at handing over the code books. He just couldn't bring himself to do it and, in any case, they were in the hands of the cypher clerk.

Cynthia then tried to persuade him to instruct the cypher clerk to hand them over to show the Admiral's good faith and enable him to return to the United States in due course.

The Admiral didn't feel that he could do that either. But he gave Cynthia the cypher clerk's name and told her that he was staying at the Shoreham Hotel.

When Cynthia tracked him down there, on the pretext, as a journalist, of wanting to interview him, he stressed that he was not just in charge of the cyphers. He declared, self-importantly, that he had broader responsibilities in the embassy.

He too was asked by Cynthia if he wanted to return to the US after the War. She could guarantee him the right to do so. She was a friend of the Admiral and knew that the old code books were due to be replaced. He would be handsomely rewarded if he could give them to her as a gesture of friendship to the neutral United States. As they were due to be replaced anyway, it could do no harm for him to do this.

He turned out to be keen both on enriching himself and on returning to the United States.

In return for $12,000, one code book was handed over forthwith and retrieved by me from Cynthia. A second book had to be extracted from him for several thousand more dollars over an expensive lunch. With Cynthia plying him with champagne and promising him favourable treatment after the War, he kept exclaiming, 'This is the life!' before handing the code book over in an ordinary shopping bag.

Once photographed, each book was despatched across

the Atlantic in the care of a King's Messenger. Our cryptographers at Bletchley Park, who had been working hard, to good effect, on the Italian codes, could not believe their luck. Stephenson received a letter of thanks from the head cryptographer, Dilly Knox. Although they were being replaced, Stephenson was told that possession of the books would help his team in checking, against earlier Italian signals, that they were on the right track in the efforts they were making to unscramble the Italian codes.

THE BATTLE OF CAPE MATAPAN

It was quite shortly afterwards, at the end of March 1941, that the news came in of the Battle of Cape Matapan, in which Admiral Cunningham scored a decisive victory over the Italian fleet in the eastern Mediterranean. As the Italian ships, as demanded by their German allies, sailed out to help counter British operations in Greece, signals about their movements were decrypted at Bletchley. When Cunningham intercepted them, an Italian battleship was damaged, three heavy cruisers and two destroyers were sunk and 2,300 Italian sailors lost their lives. The naval officer commanding the searchlights on the battleship *Valiant*, which he used to illuminate the Italian ships that night, was the youthful Prince Philip of

Greece, later the Duke of Edinburgh. Cunningham subsequently appeared personally at Bletchley to thank the
cryptographers for helping to make his victory possible.

As the news came through of the Italian defeat, with
such heavy casualties, Cynthia asked me to come round
to the small house we had rented for her at 3027 O Street
in Georgetown. I found her studying the newspapers and
looking rather pensive. Did I think her efforts had contributed to our victory? I said that I thought they probably had.

'I know what you are thinking,' she said. 'Do I feel any
remorse for having helped to send a lot of Italian sailors
to the bottom of the sea?

'The answer is that I don't. I was given an assignment
and I carried it out.

'I was given it by you,' she added, as she walked out of
the room.

Admiral Lais appeared at Cynthia's house that evening
in an even more emotional state than usual and spent the
night weeping in her arms. At first she thought this must
be because of the Italian defeat. But in the early hours
he confessed that he had received orders from Rome to
instruct their crews to scuttle all the Italian ships that had
been trapped in American ports by the British blockade.

His panic increased when two figures in the street
outside appeared to be observing the house as, because
of her association with the Admiral, J. Edgar Hoover had

confirmed an order for Cynthia to be kept ι
vation by the FBI. Having helped the Admiι
by a rear entrance on to the street behind, she ᵢ   ₐ
panic to give me this dramatic news, which I passed on
to US Naval Intelligence, well and truly establishing her
credibility with them.

By the time the US Coast Guard sought to board the
thirty Italian vessels in Norfolk, New York and elsewhere
on the eastern seaboard, all but two were in the process of
being scuttled. The Italian ambassador was informed by
the State Department that Admiral Lais, who was discovered to have given the orders for the sabotage, was 'no
longer welcome in this country'. He was declared *persona
non grata* and required to leave the US forthwith.

The Admiral asked Cynthia to spend their last night
together in the Plaza Hotel in New York. I followed in
their wake to witness his departure. The Admiral's ship,
bound for neutral Lisbon, was due to leave at 11 a.m. At
10.40 a car with the Italian Consulate's number plates
drew up on the quayside, disgorging Cynthia and the
Admiral. Only a few minutes remained before the gang-
way was raised. These were spent by them in a passionate
embrace. A ship's officer had to detach the Admiral from
Cynthia and lead him on board.

As she turned back towards the car from the Consulate, I asked the driver of my unmarked car to pull up
alongside her, opened the door and invited her to get in.

This she did, with a huge smile. Some moments were devoted to wiping away the lipstick smeared across her face, followed by what sounded like a sigh of relief.

'You didn't believe that I could do it, did you?' she declared triumphantly.

'Absolutely not,' I replied, 'and nor did anyone else.'

'Does it matter that the code books are being replaced?' she asked.

I said that I thought not. I did not believe that Cynthia's efforts had been decisive – for months Bletchley had been conducting their own attacks on the Italian naval Enigma – but Knox confirmed to me subsequently that in his opinion they had contributed to it and also to subsequent operations against the Italians in the Mediterranean, including in frustrating their attempts to interfere with our convoys to Malta. For his technique, known as 'rodding', depended in part on precisely targeted, inspired guesswork. She had not been responsible for the intercept that revealed the change of direction of the Italian fleet that had enabled Cunningham to intercept them, but the ability to read recent prior Italian naval communications had helped in guiding the 'rodding' decyphering process.

BREAKING THE RULES

I drove her back to her hotel. It was time for a celebration, I said. I would pick her up at 8.30 p.m.

I was struck by the absence of any apparent regret for the sudden departure of her boyfriend.

After the War, the Admiral's family insisted furiously that he had not betrayed any secrets; and it is true that he had refused to hand over the code books. Nevertheless, indisputably, and thanks to Cynthia, we had ended up with the cypher books, which were handed over by the cypher clerk.

When I collected her that evening, Cynthia clearly was in the mood to enjoy herself. Arriving at El Morocco, she had no difficulty turning most heads in the room as, a rope of pearls around her neck, she was barely clad in a silver dress that fitted her like a second skin. A bottle of champagne disappeared rapidly. Far from waiting until the end of dinner, we chose to dance between the courses, alone on the dance floor, to the excellent swing band.

Cynthia was an accomplished dancer and, to her surprise, I proved to be quite good too. It was a skill I had cultivated in my youth. For it had dawned on me that most of my male counterparts seemed too afraid or embarrassed to dance, while most girls were keen to do so. This had served me well in the past, including with my wife, whose family had felt that she was much too well bred for me.

As we spun around the floor, she pressed herself against me, in a disconcerting fashion. We stayed quite late. I asked the driver to take us to my hotel, the Carlyle. We clung to one another in the lift, oblivious to the bell boy taking us up to the twenty-ninth floor. In the room, we tried more champagne, then walked out to admire the lights of the city, before tumbling into bed together.

It should have come as no surprise that Cynthia liked to be on top, enthusiastically climbing all over me.

There followed next morning a repeat performance, after which Cynthia took a time out with one of her beloved cigarettes.

'Well,' she said, 'you're not so buttoned up after all.'

'No one could stay buttoned up with you,' was my reply.

For several weeks Cynthia and I continued our trysts, trying to be as discreet as we could, but generally ending up at her house on O Street or in my apartment at the Shoreham Hotel. Cynthia, of course, was not her real name (which was Elizabeth Thorpe) and nor was she a natural blonde. Her hair was light brown-ish, coloured blonde-ish by her. Her Virginia friends all called her Betty. But, however private the circumstances, she was always Cynthia to me.

In this period, when we still didn't know each other very well, I asked her if the Polish cavalry officer had been the love of her life. This produced a snort from Cynthia. 'He was every bit as much a fascist as the Germans,' she said. In his uniform, he had looked more glamorous and interesting than her husband, with whom she had become increasingly bored. She agreed to go for riding lessons with him. One of these had ended at a cabin in the forest, with a lunch of champagne and caviar, following which he had torn off her clothes and forced himself on her, a performance he had repeated in her house a few days later.

He then boasted to all his friends that she had become his mistress – hence the scandal, which had worsened when, extremely drunk, he had lunged at her at an embassy garden party. Her friend, Colonel Shelley, had thrown him out.

Finally, he had tried to see her again the day before he left to join his regiment on the German border, shouting through the locked door at her that when war broke out he was going to be killed. After she had left and the invasion took place, his armoured car squadron had been decimated by German tanks and he had not survived.

'End of story,' concluded Cynthia.

But she confessed that she had been much more interested in the good-looking *chef de cabinet* of the Polish Foreign Minister. The greater the flow of information, which she passed on to MI6, the more enthusiastic she became about him. It seemed clear that what Cynthia loved above all was the glamour and sheer excitement of being a secret agent.

* * *

Disaster then struck, in the form of a letter from my wife, announcing that now that the children were a bit older and could be cared for by her mother, she would be coming for a couple of months to join me in Washington. It was pretty clear that someone in the embassy must have told her about Cynthia. Caroline was able to hitch a lift on an RAF transport plane on its outward journey to the US.

Her arrival led Cynthia forthwith to declare a business-only relationship with me. Our occasional meetings, to which I had always looked forward so eagerly, became truly agonising for me. A renewed effort by Cynthia to undermine a political secretary in the German embassy was getting nowhere. 'Even if I had an affair with him, his pillow talk would be about the genius of the Führer,' she declared. She turned her attention instead to that of the Vichy French.

During this period of estrangement between us, Cynthia reported that she had been visited by someone who had presented himself as a colleague of mine from BSC in New York. She had invited him over for a martini at her house. She had found him very likeable and had asked him about my boss, Stephenson. 'A terrible fellow,' he had replied, 'very demanding.' She had invited him to stay in the spare room, but he had to hurry back to Washington.

As her visitor had a Canadian accent, she wondered if this had not been Stephenson himself – which, of course, it was.

*　*　*

Not long after the Battle of Cape Matapan, Admiral Godfrey and Ian Fleming appeared in Washington on a mission engineered by Stephenson. He had been cultivating the First World War hero and confidant of Roosevelt, Colonel 'Wild Bill' Donovan. During his two visits to Britain, made at Roosevelt's behest, Donovan had, literally, been entertained royally, having been invited to lunch with the King, plus numerous meetings with Churchill. His reports about British defiance had served to neutralise those of the defeatist American ambassador, Joseph Kennedy.

To be fair to the Kennedys, his sentiments were not shared by his sons, John Kennedy and his elder brother, who later was killed in the War. The paterfamilias had been sent to London by Roosevelt to get him out of the United States. He would have done better to stick to his private affairs, where his girlfriends included the actress Gloria Swanson.

Stephenson's ambition was to see Donovan crowned as the future head of US intelligence. The United States was totally unprepared for war and, prior to Pearl Harbor, had no intention of directly engaging in it. The Army, Navy and Air Force all had rudimentary intelligence divisions, as did the FBI. There was no central intelligence organisation at all. The Navy had a limited cryptanalysis function which, before Pearl Harbor, intercepted messages indicating a Japanese intention to attack (though not the target), but failed to process these fast enough to be of any use. Roosevelt was persuaded to appoint Donovan initially to be the coordinator of information, a step towards his appointment after Pearl Harbor as head of the Office of Strategic Services (OSS).

Stephenson had succeeded in helping to install his and our friend at the centre of the future US intelligence system. Hoover regarded the new set-up as a cat's paw of the Brits – a huge underestimate of Donovan. The first office of OSS was established under Allen Dulles in the Rockefeller Plaza, a few floors above BSC.

Admiral Godfrey was effusive about Cynthia's exploits. Ian Fleming was complimentary about them too. Needless to say, however, his main objective was to meet her; an idea vetoed by me.

* * *

Matapan was followed by instructions to me from Godfrey and Dilly Knox to do whatever we could to help get hold of the Vichy French naval codes, a demand that became more urgent after Pearl Harbor and the United States entered the War, as the first thoughts started to be entertained of a possible landing by the Allies in Vichy-controlled North Africa.

To Stephenson's annoyance, he too received a peremptory telegram from Menzies that it was of the utmost importance for us to acquire copies of the French codes.

'And how the hell does he think we are going to do that?' Stephenson wanted to know.

By now I found, to my amusement and mild irritation, everyone in BSC in New York wanted to know Cynthia. Her main contacts there were the very helpful Marion de Chastelain and 'Mr Howard', the pseudonym of John Pepper, but Stephenson was clear that I was to remain her controller at the sharp end, in Washington.

'I don't see how she can perform the same miracle twice. But at least let's try,' was his instruction to me.

Cynthia started at the top by asking, as a reporter, for a meeting with the French ambassador, who, however, turned out to be the most unpleasant kind of Vichy supporter. He was totally unrepentant about ever closer collaboration with the Germans, which he proclaimed to be a vital interest for France. But the meeting had been arranged for her by the press attaché, Charles Brousse. Before long, she informed me, she was getting on famously with him. A minor nobleman who was already on his third marriage, he regarded himself as an expert on food and wine and, by extension, women. Twenty years older than her, he had won the Croix de Guerre as a pilot, flying over the German trenches, in the First World War and he co-owned regional newspapers in south-west France. He had remained, at the outset, loyal to Vichy and still was reverential about Marshal Pétain, as a former war hero, but he was contemptuous of the Prime

Minister, Pierre Laval, whom he regarded as a jumped-up commercial traveller.

Cynthia warned me that Charles had a particular detestation for the British in general and the Royal Navy in particular. This was because, on 3 July 1940, Admiral Somerville had sailed into the bay of Mers-el-Kébir, where a French fleet, now under Vichy control, was at anchor. On Churchill's instructions, Somerville gave the French commander half an hour to bring his ships out of Vichy control or to scuttle them. When this ultimatum expired, Somerville was under orders to destroy the fleet, which, though personally unhappy about his orders, he did. A thousand French sailors were killed.

This spectacular act of ruthlessness had its effect in Washington, convincing Roosevelt, notwithstanding the views of Joseph Kennedy, that we were determined to continue the War. But several of Charles's friends and classmates had gone down with the French ships. He would, said Cynthia, never forgive us for this. She had to present herself as working for the Americans, as she had done before.

Charles, by this time, was more disposed to be helpful, as he discovered that Pétain was being elbowed aside by Laval. The very obvious problem was that, as press attaché, Charles could tell her all about gossip in the embassy but had little access to any sensitive information, let alone the codes.

Following the return of my wife to England, relations

had remained distant with Cynthia. But following Pearl Harbor, I took her to dinner at the Hay–Adams Hotel to celebrate the United States' entrance into the War. I had chosen the venue carefully, as a string trio playing music in a corner gave me the opportunity to invite her to dance.

Cynthia was so excited that we were now fully paid-up allies that she decided to overcome her reservations about me, even though I suspected that by now she probably already was entangled with her French Count. Hoping for the best, I already had the key to a room in the hotel and the rest of the evening passed as if there had never been any distance between us.

*   *   *

As plans advanced in 1942 for the possible invasion of North Africa, the need to get hold, if we could, of the Vichy naval codes was becoming more urgent by the week. Cynthia knew nothing of the planned landings but needed no convincing of the urgency.

This led her to make, without consulting me or Charles, a really serious mistake. As Charles had no access to the codes, she invited another French attaché – also a minor nobleman – who supervised the cypher office, to meet her in an apartment we had rented for her in the Wardman Park Hotel. She 'confessed' that she was working for US intelligence. Though she claimed that she had made no mention of the naval codes, she said that he would be well rewarded if he could enlighten her about Vichy naval plans. He said that he would think this over.

Although he seemed understandably keen to see her again, her instinct warned her that this approach probably had misfired.

Back in his embassy, the attaché told the Vichy ambassador that he had been approached by a beautiful American spy, who had asked him to betray French naval secrets. Heroically, he had resisted this approach.

Hearing from his colleague about this assignation, Charles slapped her so hard that she had to hide behind huge dark glasses for several days.

I felt like doing so myself, particularly as the French ambassador then complained to the State Department about the approach to his attaché.

A BURGLARY LIKE NO OTHER

Charles, however, by this time, was thoroughly disillusioned with Vichy, though he still had reservations about de Gaulle. Cynthia by now had told him that she worked for US intelligence. As our investigations had shown that Charles was quite wealthy in property in France but had very little in his US bank account, she offered him a monthly subsidy, ostensibly from her US colleagues.

In response, he gave Cynthia decyphered copies of a telegram from the Vichy naval commander Admiral

Darlan demanding a report on the locations of the British naval vessels in US ports and of the embassy's reply, which Darlan no doubt intended to pass on to the Germans. Meanwhile, BSC in New York had started using their excellent US media contacts to mount a press campaign against the Vichy embassy in Washington.

Following Pearl Harbor, with America now in the War, Cynthia asked Charles directly for his help in acquiring the Vichy French naval cyphers. His objections were purely practical. The cyphers were so closely held and well protected that he considered the task to be impossible. But he provided Cynthia with details of the layout of the embassy, showing that the cypher room with the naval codes was next to the naval attaché's office on the raised ground floor.

With the US now our allies, the OSS allocated a Colonel Ellery Huntington to operations against the Vichy embassy. I introduced him to Cynthia, who arranged for him to meet Charles, verifying her story about her working for US intelligence.

We had ruled out the idea of a burglary as simply too difficult as the embassy at night was patrolled by a security officer who took his job seriously. But Cynthia said that if the Stephenson operation had a really competent burglar on their books, she would like to discuss the problem with him.

The answer, of course, was that they did. Cynthia was taken to New York and introduced to an American burglar who claimed to be at the very top of his profession. He had helped BSC to steal documents from several consulates in New York and was especially skilled in decyphering the combinations to safes.

He warned, however, that unravelling the combination to a really well-protected safe required patience. It could take hours; and in this case he would need to crack the combination to the door to the cypher room as well as that to the safe in which the books were held. More time would then be required to photograph them. How was this to be achieved when the embassy was constantly patrolled?

It was Cynthia who came up with a possible solution to this apparently insoluble problem.

She had a series of intense discussions with Charles about how to bamboozle the night watchman, with the two of them concluding that one of her schemes just possibly might work.

Her plan was for Charles to tell his colleague that he was having an affair with her. This had to be conducted very discreetly, as he was still married. He proposed to bring his lady friend, plus champagne and a light meal, into the embassy after hours. They would have supper in the embassy's waiting room, which conveniently had a large divan. If the security guard would cooperate, he would be well rewarded by Charles (financed through her by us).

Charles agreed to try this out, taking Cynthia and a

hamper of food and wine with him to the embassy, well after hours, having forewarned the guard of his plans. The guard, keen on the promised reward, had declared himself to be a man of the world who was willing to help his colleague in an affair of the heart (a very Latin reaction – I couldn't see such a scheme having much chance of working with one of our own less gallant guards).

The guard, as promised, stayed away from the entrance area and the waiting room and seemed to spend much of his time relaxing on an upper floor. This stratagem was repeated on a second occasion.

On their third assignation, Charles and Cynthia asked him to join them for a celebratory glass of champagne, laced by Cynthia with a sedative, Nembutal. When all seemed quiet, the BSC burglar entered the building, admitted by Charles. Cynthia guided him to the steel door of the cypher room. There followed over two hours of nerve-racking tension as he struggled with the combination. When this finally was mastered, he showed Cynthia how to unlock it in future, then attempted to unlock the safe. Time was running out by the time he had at last succeeded in doing so. There was no time to photograph the cypher books and they then had to withdraw. But the operation had not been detected.

The next attempt was made a week later with Cynthia, who had been given the combination to the safe, entrusted with opening it. But when Cynthia tried, the safe wouldn't open.

After she reported this to me, Cynthia was summoned to New York for a meeting with our burglar in a truck in which he had installed a replica of the safe. He taught Cynthia how to 'feel' the combination and to wait to hear the tumblers fall into place after each turn of the dial. She had been trying to do it all too fast.

This had been arranged by John Pepper in New York because he feared that if the burglar were arrested in the embassy he could incriminate BSC, while Cynthia's presence could be explained away.

But the BSC staff in New York, who were nowhere near the action, did not appear to have any idea of the strain Cynthia would be under during this operation. She was extremely unhappy about making a final attempt to photograph the code books without the burglar and I wholeheartedly agreed with her. So I got his subordinates overruled by Stephenson.

Charles once again told the guard in advance that he must not be disturbed. To Cynthia's relief, the burglar was able to be let in through the window to the waiting room. But she was troubled that the guard had not appeared to greet them, as he had done on the previous occasions. Her instinct told her to take some additional precautions. While the burglar worked, this time quickly, to open the safe, Cynthia stood at the entrance to the waiting room, close to the corridor leading to the cypher room, and removed all her clothes, ending up wearing only her pearls and high-heeled shoes. She also told Charles to get at least partly undressed.

It was just as well that she did, as the watchman suddenly appeared, waving his torch around. Having caught a glimpse of her undressed – and, in a real, not simulated, panic, exclaiming 'Oh la la!' – he switched it off with profuse apologies, staying away thereafter.

If we had attempted this operation without the burglar, the evidently suspicious watchman might have found Cynthia struggling with the safe.

The books were despatched with the burglar to be photographed in a suite Colonel Huntington had arranged in the Wardman Park Hotel. With Charles and Cynthia in a state of high anxiety, the code books were not brought back until 5 a.m., but the operation had remained undetected.

While this had not been an OSS operation, apart from the photography, after the War Cynthia was amused, though also delighted, to find herself being portrayed by American writers as the Mata Hari of OSS.

The negatives of the copies of the code books were handed over by Huntington to US Naval Intelligence and despatched to Bletchley in the care of a King's Messenger on an RAF aircraft. I received effusive thanks from Dilly Knox and congratulations from Stephenson, for both of whom Cynthia by now had achieved legendary status.

The landings in North Africa took place at the end of the year. The US Navy sank Vichy French ships and bombarded the shore batteries in a battle off Casablanca. The naval operation and subsequent landings had been aided by the signals intelligence to which, this time Dilly Knox confirmed to me, Cynthia had made a decisive contribution, far more directly than at Matapan, as the naval codes she had acquired enabled the instant decyphering of the messages sent to and from Admiral Darlan, commanding the Vichy forces in North Africa.

The intercepts had revealed the state and dispositions of the Vichy naval defences, the crumbling of the Vichy defenders' morale during the conflict and the precise moment at which they might be prepared to sue for peace. To Charles's utter disgust (and that of Churchill), after several days' fighting, in which 500 Allied soldiers and three times as many Vichy French were killed, Eisenhower did a deal with the detestable Darlan whereby the Vichy forces would cease resistance if he were left in place. This problem fortunately was solved when Darlan was assassinated by a French monarchist who, sadly, was executed, rather than decorated, for ridding us of him.

On behalf of OSS, Cynthia was told formally by Colonel Huntington, who had participated in the landings in North Africa himself, that her efforts 'had saved a lot of Allied soldiers' lives'. This was repeated to her verbatim by Bill Donovan, the head of OSS, who later showed his appreciation by intervening personally to help her to get together with Charles, who had been interned as, ostensibly, a Vichy supporter.

Dilly sadly died a year later, two years before the end of the War, which he and his colleagues made such a huge contribution to winning.

*   *   *

I had by now ended my peroration at the Alibi Club, concluding with Cynthia in a state of undress to distract the guard while we hijacked the Vichy French naval codes and ending with the successful landings in North Africa. It was greeted with a round of applause.

'What an amazing woman!' someone exclaimed.

Dulles said that Cynthia was now living in France. 'I believe that she has retired, though only our friend here would really know,' he added with a smile.

I wanted all of you to hear this story, as a demonstration that, in our profession, it sometimes is feasible to achieve the apparently impossible, as Kim did in Iran. Who on earth could have imagined that one agent could steal the naval codes of two hostile powers? Who could have imagined that the head of the *Abwehr* would end up on our side?

You may be thinking that we shall not see her like again. But to defeat the Soviets, which we will, we are going to have to find some more like her. What was extraordinary about her was her absolute determination to succeed in her mission, plus a streak of ruthlessness, which also has been the hallmark of most of the really successful men I know. I don't know where we will find another Cynthia, but I am sure that we will, perhaps in the unlikeliest of places. It is your job to find someone who can do the apparently impossible for us all over again.

I thought I understood what he was hinting at. For SIS in Moscow had established the first contacts with a Colonel in the scientific department of Soviet Military Intelligence (the 'Main Directorate' – the GRU). A war veteran, he was a friend of Ivan Serov, head of the GRU. His contact was with a British businessman in Moscow, Greville Wynne, but all intelligence from him was shared with the CIA. We did not yet know how important Colonel Oleg Penkovsky was going to prove to be. Other, far less important Soviet agents had defected to us outside the Soviet Union. There had, hitherto, been only one worthwhile defector, of lower rank, from the GRU in Moscow. Penkovsky was in a much more important position. This was, potentially, our first really major breakthrough there.

'YOU'RE NO GOOD AT MARRIAGE'

Following the landings, Charles started pressing to join the Free French in North Africa, but was talked out of this by Cynthia and OSS had other ideas for him.

Cynthia and I had been continuing our periodic short

getaways to New York, where we stayed in a hotel by Gramercy Park and explored the cafes and restaurants around Union Square. We had to be discreet as Charles, from every point of view, would have been very upset to learn of her relationship with me. Nevertheless, we always seemed to end up dancing at El Morocco.

It was at this point, when things were looking much better in the War, that Cynthia dropped her bombshell. She had decided to marry Charles. Although I had feared as much, I still could scarcely believe it. We had experienced so much together and, partly because they were so episodic, our interludes together were so intense that I had refused to believe that things might come to this.

'Don't be so dismayed,' she said. 'The fact is, you're no good at marriage. You scarcely even know the names of your children. You're always going to be a better bet as a lover, at any rate with me.'

As I absorbed this shattering news, I protested feebly that Charles had been hopeless as a husband too. She was confident that she could cure that (and she did). He wanted to settle down. She doubted if I did. 'And anyway, you didn't ask me.'

Thereby she left me wondering why on earth I didn't.

Cynthia moved in with Charles, whose divorce took for ever to come through. They did not in fact get married until the very end of the War.

Predictably, however, she was getting bored. Without telling me, she asked Stephenson to help to get her sent into occupied France. She claimed to him that she spoke good French, which was true, but she was not fluent enough to enable her to pass as a local. Stephenson sent her name forward to the SOE but then consulted me.

I asked him to withdraw it forthwith, which he did. I knew the head of the French division of SOE, Colonel Maurice Buckmaster, who, in my opinion, was an excessively gung-ho soldier. I knew, from my naval colleagues in London, that he had sent agents into France in circumstances where most of them were betrayed shortly after landing, with many of the reception parties penetrated by informers, and precious few of them survived.

Violette Szabo was dropped into France two days after the Normandy landings, only for her to be captured immediately, sent to Ravensbrück and executed there. After the War, Buckmaster's assistant Vera Atkins spent years trying to trace the hundred-plus agents, including fourteen women, who had simply disappeared. The landing officer in France for Buckmaster's operations turned out to have been a German agent.

OSS then hatched their own plan, which was to ask Charles to continue to pretend to be loyal to Vichy. When the French embassy was closed down in Washington, the Vichy staff were sent into comfortable detention at the Greenbrier resort in West Virginia. Donovan instructed the FBI to let Cynthia join him there (under the pretence that she was his daughter!). Their idea was to send Cynthia and Charles together into occupied France, pretending that Charles was still a Vichy supporter. I frustrated this plan too by pointing out that, by this time, Cynthia was too well known to have been a British and American agent.

Cynthia, of course, found out what I had done, making quite a scene.

It was not until June 1944 that I received a different kind of telephone call from her. 'Do you remember our celebration after Pearl Harbor and the US entered the War?' she enquired. Of course I did, I replied. 'Don't you think we should do something to celebrate the landings in France?'

I went ahead to New York, booking us into the Carlyle. We spent the next two days happily together, dancing again at El Morocco. Someone recognised her there, but she didn't seem to care; and nor did I.

*   *   *

These occasional escapades continued after the end of the War. For Charles, now married to Cynthia, had moved back to France, where he was devoting himself to restoring an ancient and beautiful castle in the foothills of the Pyrenees. Cynthia found it very romantic at first though, to keep themselves warm amidst the thick stone walls, log fires had to be lit even in the summer. I smiled at the thought of Cynthia as a chatelaine, but, speaking good French and taking her role very seriously, she proved pretty good at it and popular with the neighbours. In the summer, they visited the beautiful old fishing villages of Collioure, beloved of Matisse and Derain, and S'Agaró, across the Spanish border. But, she told Charles, she could not spend all her time in the cold and windy Pyrenees. She needed to meet people and to breathe some fresh oxygen. So, twice a year, she travelled back to Virginia.

I had been summoned back to Naval Intelligence in London, where I was no longer upstaged by Ian Fleming, who had a distinguished record in intelligence in the War though, as he himself lamented, nearly all of it at head-quarters and none of it in the field. He had concluded, rightly, that his expensive lifestyle could not be sustained on the pay of an intelligence officer, so he opted instead for a much, much better-paid post in journalism with the Kemsley Press, owners of the *Sunday Times*. So, thanks to Cynthia, I was now pretty much the star of the department. The assignment permitted me to return to Washington from time to time for liaison with my counterparts in US Naval Intelligence and liaisons in New York with Cynthia.

A DRINK WITH PHILBY

In the course of one of these visits, I was invited for a drink at his house on Nebraska Avenue by the new representative in Washington of SIS, Kim Philby. I knew about him by repute as a rapidly rising star, the blue-eyed boy of Stewart Menzies and, supposedly, the only member of SIS (at the time still mostly a bunch of amateurs) who understood the Soviet Union. In fact, much of his reputation was based on his expertise on Communism (though I doubt if he ever struggled through Marx's dense tome *Capital*, which I also had failed to do).

A more junior colleague, Carew Hunt, had written the SIS handbook on *The Theory and Practice of Communism*. Unsurprisingly, however, he had proved no match for Philby in discussing the subject.

This may well be coloured by retrospect, but I did not take to Kim, though I had been assured that I would find him erudite and very charming. He had, I was told, made a good start in Washington through his well-advertised friendship with the part English-educated James Angleton of the CIA, whom he had mentored when an OSS team first arrived in London during the War. But Philby's would-be ingratiating manner, with his hesitancy and slight stammer, seemed affected to me.

He had started by expressing his unbounded admiration for my achievements with Cynthia. 'How can any of us ever compete with that?' he enquired. He was, of course, in due course to outdo me, but in a different cause. He then asked about my exchanges with my US counterparts. How worried were they about the new planned Soviet nuclear submarines? How did they estimate their capabilities? How did they plan to counter this threat? 'By building more and better ones themselves,' was my reply.

I attached at the time little importance to this encounter, beyond irritation that the SIS representative seemed to have ambitions to supervise the work of other intelligence departments.

Some time afterwards, he tracked down Cynthia who, despite his reputed success with women, also did not take to him. He seemed both bitter and envious about you, she told me. He expressed surprise that she had chosen to work for us rather than the US. 'I had to remind him that America was neutral at the time,' she snorted. He also had asked why we had not got married. 'Because I didn't want to,' was her reply.

ATOM SPIES

In London I became a member of the Joint Intelligence Committee, bringing together the representatives of all the intelligence services, which introduced me to the senior members of MI5, who could not have been more different in character to 'those prima donnas', which was the kindest term they had for their thoroughly disliked, attention-seeking rivals in MI6. For these were men of a different ilk, non-commissioned officers rather than officers, many of whom had been involved in policing subversion (later known as 'liberation') in the colonies.

In the early years after the War, our main preoccupation was with the atom spies. Alan Nunn May was a

Cambridge physicist and Communist who was transferred with other Cambridge physicists to work on a heavy-water reactor in Canada. He supplied his Soviet contacts with samples of the radioactive isotopes Uranium-233 and 235. The courier who handled them, we learned later, needed lifelong blood transfusions to counter the radioactivity he had absorbed.

Transferred back to London at the end of the War, Nunn May arranged to meet his Soviet handler outside the British Museum. But his work for the Soviets was revealed by a GRU cypher clerk in Ottawa, Igor Gouzenko, who defected to the Canadians in September 1945. Nunn May was arrested outside the British Museum and sentenced to ten years' hard labour.

Klaus Fuchs, who was arrested and convicted five years later, was a German refugee physicist whose parents were Communists; he had earned a doctorate from the University of Edinburgh. MI5 had noted on his file that he had been a Communist in Germany. Yet, because he was so strongly recommended as a brilliant physicist by a key leader of our nuclear research team, Rudolf Peierls, also of German origin but loyal to the Allies, it was concluded, unbelievably, that employing Fuchs on what turned into the British atomic Tube Alloys programme was 'a risk worth taking'.

With his colleagues, he then moved on to work on the Manhattan Project at Los Alamos as an expert on implosion, which was critical to the development of a plutonium bomb. The War over, he returned to the UK Atomic Energy Research Establishment at Harwell.

It was a reference to him in the Venona intercepts of Soviet intelligence communications that led to his interrogation in 1950, in the course of which he confessed to having been a Soviet agent from day one. Having served his sentence, he migrated to his natural home in East Germany.

So we had accounted, very belatedly, for our two main atom spies but not, to my regret, for Melita Norwood. For though she was unable to do nearly as much damage in her role in the British Non-Ferrous Metals Research Association, it was not for any lack of trying.

Although we knew about her, it was decided not to bother prosecuting her as it would not be worth the embarrassment it would cause.

My task and that of my colleagues was to help ensure a drastic strengthening of the disastrously lax, virtually non-existent security vetting procedures which had permitted Nunn May and Fuchs to inflict the damage they had done, and our efforts to do so met with some success.

Fortunately for our relationship with them, the Americans had discovered a contingent of atom spies of their own. Highest on the list were Julius and Ethel Rosenberg. They had met as members of the Young Communist League in New York and Ethel's brother, David Greenglass, who had recruited others to the cause, turned state's evidence against them. From various positions in the US defence industry and via the agents they recruited, they were convicted of having supplied the Soviet Union with top-secret information about radar, sonar, jet engines and nuclear weapons design. Found guilty of espionage, both were due to be sent to the electric chair.

There was a huge outcry in Europe, with Sartre, Picasso, Cocteau, Einstein and almost every intellectual I had ever heard of arguing that they were innocent or at least they should be spared. As the British press were taking the same line, I was despatched across the Atlantic to see what, if anything, could be done. I was given short shrift by my contacts, as the Venona transcripts, which could not be used in court, showed that the Rosenbergs were as guilty as sin. Eisenhower refused to commute the sentences.

I also was asked to make enquiries about what was seen as the 'persecution' of J. Robert Oppenheimer. Having made a vital contribution to the development of the atom bomb, Oppenheimer by now was expressing remorse for having done so. I found my colleagues in the CIA less sympathetic to him than I had expected. One erudite cynic observed that his position was like that of Saint Augustine: 'Please make me virtuous, Oh Lord, but not yet,' and certainly not until after he had become famous. The FBI took me through the long list of his friends and research associates who were, or had been, Communists. I was able to report to London that they did not intend to prosecute him but they were determined to revoke his security clearance. For, no doubt for idealistic reasons, he believed that, in the interests of world peace, America's nuclear secrets must be shared with the Soviet Union.

As Hoover's deputy observed to me, this was after Stalin's purges, the massacre in 1940 by the Russians of over 20,000 Polish military and police officers and other potential opponents, mostly in the forest at Katyn, and the subjugation of Eastern Europe. 'How naïve can you get?' The Katyn massacre had been revealed during the War by the Poles in exile. These facts, in his view, were ignored by half the Western intelligentsia *because they did not want to know*. His fellow scientist Edward Teller was among those who contended that Oppenheimer's security clearance must be withdrawn, which it was.

BURGESS AND MACLEAN

One day in early 1951, I was summoned to an especially secret meeting at the MI5 headquarters, about which I was told, on pain of death, I must tell no one else. This, it turned out, was to discuss the head of the American Department in the Foreign Office, with whom I had overlapped in the Washington embassy, Donald Maclean. I recalled him as an immensely tall, languid individual, who took great pride in the fact that his father had been a Cabinet Minister and seemed the sort of supremely snobbish British establishment figure I most disliked.

His wife, Melinda, was a New York socialite (who, once they were all in Moscow together, later decamped with Philby).

As I listened to the story, I could not believe that he was still in any sort of government position at all. For in his previous posting, in the British embassy in Cairo, Maclean had suffered 'some sort of breakdown'. In a drunken rage, he had trashed the flat of two girls from the American embassy. Yet, when he was brought back to London, after a period of medical 'rest' and treatment, he had been appointed head of the American department in the Foreign Office. Across his desk there passed a vast amount of material about our relations with the United States.

With a signals intelligence expert present, I was told that their US counterparts had succeeded in decrypting a Soviet intelligence telegram revealing the existence of a Soviet spy in the British embassy in Washington. I knew full well that they must have intercepted far more than just one telegram and that this no doubt was another item from the Venona intercepts.

At first, the mole was thought to be a locally employed member of the embassy staff. But a further decyphered message had revealed that the agent, codenamed 'Homer', had a wife who, while pregnant, had been staying with her mother in New York, which had been the case with Melinda.

I could only tell them that, in my limited experience of him, I had no reason to believe that Maclean was a Soviet agent. My colleagues in MI5 and signals intelligence were convinced that he was. But as I was told over and over again thereafter, in this case and others, the intercepts could not be used in court and, without them, Maclean would not be convicted. So he was placed under surveillance by MI5 in the hope that he would incriminate himself.

There followed another amazing blunder. MI5 had no love for Philby as he had suggested that there was no need for separate representation by them in Washington; he could do both jobs himself. There was no imperative need for Philby to know about the surveillance of Maclean. Yet, fatally, he was told about it and arranged for Burgess to warn Maclean to escape to Moscow.

Guy Burgess was an Old Etonian, socially well connected, including with Victor Rothschild, and had friends in the London intelligentsia. Like Philby, Anthony Blunt and John Cairncross, he had been at Trinity College, Cambridge, though they were not all there at the same time; and Maclean was at Trinity Hall. Given his personal habits, he should never have been employed by the government in any capacity. But no one had bothered to look into those. During the War, he had been recruited for MI6 by Blunt.

On checking, I discovered that Burgess had never undergone any serious vetting whatsoever. The Russians themselves turned out to have had their doubts about his dependability – as a spy! A frequently drunken aggressive homosexual, goodness knows why he had ever been sent to Washington, where he had disgraced himself on several different occasions.

Philby had invited his friend to stay with him in Nebraska Avenue, in the vain hope that this would help to keep him under control. When Burgess broke the speed limit spectacularly in Virginia three times in a single day, the Governor helped to ensure that he had to be recalled. This enabled Philby to ask him on his return to England to warn Maclean, though urging him not to defect as well, as that could compromise Philby's own position.

When Burgess got to London, it was his mentor and fellow spy, Blunt, later Surveyor of the Queen's Pictures, who contacted their Soviet controller, Yuri Modin, to arrange the getaway. MI5 by this time had plenty of 'watchers', some more competent than others. But full-time surveillance of a suspect required a lot of manpower and infinite patience. After several weeks of this, MI5 ceased to monitor Maclean when he took the train back to his house in Kent. On 25 May 1951, he and Burgess escaped on the ferry to St Malo in France.

Burgess, we learned later from those who managed to contact him in Moscow, had not wanted to go. He was appalled at the prospect of life there, though the Russians did provide a boyfriend for him. But their handler Modin was concerned, with good reason, that under interrogation, Burgess would crack and incriminate Philby and Blunt, so he was told that he had to go.

Burgess and Maclean had outlived their usefulness as Soviet agents. Burgess spent his remaining years unhappily in Russia, dying mainly of alcoholism at fifty-two.

The days that followed were a horrible wake-up call for the intelligence community, of which I was part, in London. The Foreign Office hierarchy were distraught. MI5 surveillance had failed. The agency that accepted no responsibility for this disaster were Philby's employers in SIS.

The reaction in Washington was to find it incredible that anyone could doubt Philby's guilt. On the basis of a memo to him by his deputy Bill Harvey, General Bedell Smith, head of the CIA, demanded Philby's immediate recall. James Angleton wrote a dissenting memo, refusing to believe that his friend could be a spy, but the FBI had reached the same conclusion as Harvey. The Americans would have nothing more to do with Philby.

His friends and supporters in SIS were appalled at this, to them, unjustified disparagement of their shining star. For, while he was in Washington, he had been mentioned by Menzies to his colleagues as a possible future head of the service.

This had led to MI5 being commissioned to produce a report about him. This mentioned that the picture of a mole described by the Soviet defectors Walter Krivitsky and Gouzenko conceivably could apply to Philby, as well as others. From this moment on, MI5 had their doubts about him.

So, I do not believe that Philby could have risen to the very top of the service – which did not diminish the immense amount of damage he had been able to do. His devotion to the Communist cause had not been weakened by the disappearance of his first three Soviet handlers in the Stalin purges or by the 1939 Nazi–Soviet pact.

Ironically, as we discovered later, through much of the War, Philby and the other Cambridge spies were distrusted in Moscow because of their failure to report British intelligence operations in the Soviet Union due to the fact that, at the time, none were actually taking place. The Moscow Centre of the NKVD, refusing to believe this, warned its station in London that they must be double agents engaged in deception, though it was admitted that some of the information they had provided about German military dispositions had been useful. This paranoid suspicion of some of their most valuable agents unfortunately did not last. In the last two years of the War, the intelligence they provided was being hailed in Moscow as of great value.

As I was known to have maintained good relations with the Americans and still to have their confidence, I was deputed to be one of those to fly to Washington in due course to try to reassure them that the damage caused by Burgess and, particularly, Maclean would be limited and that we knew what we were doing, which I was far from certain we did.

INTERROGATION OF PHILBY

The first stages in this process were the successive interrogations of Kim Philby, part of whose defence was that if he had been guilty he would have defected like the others. To prepare for these, we had to go through all the circumstantial evidence against him, much of which had been summarised in Harvey's memo to Bedell Smith. This focused on the successive groups of anti-Communist exiles that had been betrayed and rounded up soon after they got ashore in Albania. The moving spirit behind this ill-advised venture had been Frank Wisner of the CIA, but Philby had been a co-chair of the campaign. The evidence in the Volkov case was especially damning. For when Volkov, a Soviet intelligence agent, attempted to defect to our mission in Istanbul, he had specified that there was a Soviet agent in a senior position in counter-intelligence in London. Stewart Menzies immediately had informed Philby, whose horrified response was that, having served in Turkey, he should be sent to Istanbul to bring Volkov back to London. Instead, there was a frantic burst of electronic traffic between London and the Moscow Centre and a three weeks' delay by Philby in setting off to Istanbul, during which the inert figure of Volkov, heavily bandaged and sedated, had been extracted on a flight to Moscow. Apart from his disastrous error in choosing Philby for this task, Menzies had failed to insist that Volkov must be extracted forthwith.

It was already known that Philby's first wife was a Communist, though this was deemed to have been a youthful indiscretion.

Beyond all that, there was the indication from Gouzenko about the Soviet mole who had been a British journalist, which Philby had been for *The Times*, acting as a Soviet agent during the Civil War in Spain.

Then there were traces in the Venona intercepts of references to a highly valued Soviet 'ring of five' spies, all educated at Cambridge.

There was no way Philby could deny his extremely close association with Burgess, which was what had finished him with the Americans.

I was never in the room for these interrogations and I was only present at a couple of them when I and others listened in an adjoining room. Otherwise, I listened to the tape recordings.

What was most striking about them was that most of the interrogators ended up believing what they wanted to. My friends in MI5 fumed as they heard Philby's colleagues in SIS feed him softball questions and even provide helpful suggestions for the answers.

It was difficult not grudgingly to admire Philby's performance. He had decided to brazen it out because he believed that under the UK judicial system he would not be convicted in court. (In the Soviet Union, which he so admired, he would simply have been taken out and shot.) All the evidence against him, he declared, was purely circumstantial. He had divorced his Communist wife. In the Spanish Civil War, he had received a (nominal) decoration from Franco. The Albanian exiles were hopeless about security and had been infiltrated. He had no idea what had happened to Volkov.

I listened to the recording of MI5's star interrogator, Jim Skardon, who had helped to extract a confession from Klaus Fuchs, being so bamboozled by Philby that he ended up concluding that he thought that Philby might be innocent.

But as we went through this process, it was pretty clear that Guy Liddell, more senior in MI5, did not believe Philby's explanations. I listened to Dick White, soon to become head of MI5, sounding incredulous about Philby's denials that he had warned Burgess and Maclean and furious about his failure to explain his three weeks' delay in setting out to bring back Volkov from Istanbul.

The final interrogation was carried out by a QC, 'Buster' Milmo, who concluded in exasperation that he had not the slightest doubt that Philby was guilty but, absent further evidence, this could not be proved in court.

Thanks to Milmo's report, however, and the fact that he was totally distrusted by the Americans, it was decided that Philby must be asked to resign from SIS. This still was very much against their wishes and he was awarded a severance package. Stewart Menzies remained convinced of his innocence, taking Philby out to lunch to tell him so.

But this did at least clear the way for my pilgrimage,

and that of some others, to Washington, to try to undo what damage we could.

My foray started with lunch at the Georgetown Inn with Cynthia, who did not doubt for a minute that Philby was a spy. He seemed to have developed a particular dislike of you, without even knowing you, she said. That wasn't a good sign. She also had met and couldn't stand 'that little worm Burgess'.

We agreed to meet in a week's time at the Carlyle for a few days together in New York. 'What about Charles?' I enquired. 'He is spending his time in the Pyrenees, restoring his beautiful old castle there, and I will be going back shortly. But he understands that I have to have some breaks, some time to myself,' she claimed.

Before leaving, she gave me some good advice. 'Don't be too defensive,' she declared. 'Remind them about Alger Hiss, who was with Roosevelt at Yalta.' She also knew all about Harry Dexter White, deputy head of the US Treasury, who had disliked Maynard Keynes so much that he addressed him in meetings as 'Your Royal Highness'. Cynthia, who knew Keynes, who could indeed be pompous, found this amusing. But White had been another senior Soviet spy. Tyler Kent, a cypher clerk in the US embassy in London, had handed over to the Italians, who had passed it to Admiral Canaris, head of the *Abwehr*, the entire Roosevelt/Churchill correspondence up until he was arrested in May 1940.

Then of course there were the US atomic spies, the

Rosenbergs, who had done more damage than Philby. They, however, were being sent to the electric chair, while few of our traitors were ever to suffer any consequences at all.

The case of Hiss was the most relevant. Pictured sitting immediately behind Roosevelt at Yalta, the State Department had been warned about him in 1939, in a report they had then pigeonholed. We were not the only incompetents.

BLOOD ON HIS HANDS

I set off for my meeting with Bill Harvey and some of his colleagues at the CIA headquarters, followed by lunch at his favourite restaurant, which, curiously, was called Harvey's. Burly and jowly, Harvey's appearance belied his intelligence. Particularly over lunch, he was very friendly. 'We know, of course, that you agree with us about Kim,' he said. How he knew that I agreed was not entirely clear, but I confirmed that I did. We discussed the difficulty we had on both sides of the Atlantic in rooting out the 'true believer' Communist spies, who still idolised our wartime allies the Soviets, agreeing that it would take a good many more years for the true nature of that regime to start becoming apparent to the most blinkered of them.

'We will then be back to dealing with less dangerous traitors, who do it only for the money,' he concluded.

But in the formal meeting with his colleagues, some very pointed questions had been asked about our failure to read the danger signs over Burgess and Maclean and the continued sympathy of many of his colleagues for Philby. These reflected, Harvey confirmed, the views of his boss, Bedell Smith.

The rest of the conversation took place not in the restaurant, but in the security of Harvey's car. In his view, he declared, there was a fundamental difference between Philby and all the other traitors, including the atom spies. For Philby alone had a lot of blood on his hands. Volkov and plenty of anti-Communist Albanians had been killed by him, and most of them probably were tortured before they were shot.

This made it imperative that Philby should not be allowed to get away with his crimes. 'If you can find a way to hand him over to us, we will know how to deal with him.'

While I agreed with his sentiments, I did not, I said, see a way in which we could hand him over. And even in Philby's case, we could not permit a suspect to be subjected to Soviet-style methods of interrogation.

That was not what he had in mind, Harvey replied. But in very serious cases, involving national security, the US had the ability to keep serious suspects *indefinitely* in sleep-deprived detention, which rarely failed to elicit a confession.

While I would gladly have wished this on Philby,

I pointed out that it was predominantly our national security, rather than that of the US, that had been compromised.

Ironically, next on my agenda was a drink with Philby's lone supporter in Washington, James Angleton. 'Over many years and in many difficult situations,' he declared,

> I got to know Kim Philby as well as any man I have ever known, and I'll be damned if I believe that he is a traitor. Since the end of the War, we've worked together on many schemes to frustrate the Soviets. How could that be the case if Kim was working for the other side?

What did I think? he wanted to know.

I acknowledged that nothing had been proved definitively about Philby, but his answers about the delay in retrieving Volkov had been evasive and we had to be guided by Milmo's report.

On leaving, it was clear that Angleton was self-deluding. It was simply too difficult for him to acknowledge that he, the great spymaster, as he saw himself, had been bamboozled by his friend. Nor could he ever admit that all the confidences he had shared with Philby could have ended up in the wrong hands.

Next, I moved on to FBI headquarters, where I got, as I expected, a frosty reception. There never were any diplomatic niceties or friendly luncheons with Hoover's hard-faced minions, who were at the sharp end of US law enforcement. How on earth had we ever engaged so obvious a security risk as Guy Burgess? And what did we now intend to do about Philby?

I ran through the list of prominent Americans who had proved to be Soviet spies (and whose responsibility it had been the Bureau's to track down), adding that I was prepared to bet them that in due course they would find that many more Americans had been recruited as Soviet agents than was the case in Britain. They had no answer to this, wrestling as they were with the allegations of Whittaker Chambers, himself a former Soviet agent, about the extent of Soviet penetration of the US.

The fact remained, however, that there was no easy answer to either of the questions they had asked and I must have left them with as poor an opinion about our competence as they made clear they had when I arrived.

Nevertheless, my mission was regarded as a modest success, with a brief note of thanks from Menzies, as we were now back on speaking terms with our disappointed friends in the CIA.

There followed another few days with Cynthia, by now sufficiently well known at the Carlyle for the pianist to start playing her favourite songs whenever she walked into the bar. We spent the evenings dancing in a trance and then with drinks on the terrace of our room overlooking the lights of New York.

The Philby affair had quietened down. We had been able to confirm to the Americans that, as Menzies and

I had promised, he would no longer have access to any classified information and he would be kept under observation by MI5.

'HE IS NOT THE THIRD MAN'

Menzies's successor as head of MI6, however, Major General Sir John ('Sinbad') Sinclair, was not prepared to leave it at that. Egged on by his colleagues in MI6, he kept complaining to Dick White and others that Milmo's conclusion had been reached with no hard evidence. Philby had been the victim of a 'miscarriage of justice'.

Though a journalist called Chapman Pincher with good contacts in MI5 kept making enquiries, the affair no longer figured much in the press, with most of us hoping that it would stay that way. All hopes of it doing so were well and truly upset no less than four years later by J. Edgar Hoover, who, outraged that we had not found a way to lock Philby up, planted in the *New York Sunday News* the story that he had been identified as the 'third man'.

This placed the government in a hopeless position, as they had no usable evidence to prove this. The allegations caused a storm in the press and were raised in Parliament by a Labour MP called Marcus Lipton.

I was not consulted about the Foreign Secretary's reply, but SIS were, including those who had recruited Philby to the service and were firm believers in his innocence. So, to my amazement and that of MI5, the Foreign Secretary, Harold Macmillan, stood up in Parliament to assert that Philby was not the 'third man, if indeed there was one'. What he should have said was that there was no proof that he was.

So Philby was able to hold a triumphant press conference, proclaiming that his innocence had now been confirmed on the highest authority. The last time he had spoken to a Communist, knowing that he was a Communist, he declared, had been in 1934. He had been asked to resign from the Foreign Office because of an 'imprudent association' (with Burgess). He had not known that Burgess was a Communist. His conduct had been deplorable.

Philby and his Soviet handlers could not have been more exultant, while his friends in SIS were just as triumphant too.

I told one of the leaders of this gang that I was damned-well certain that Philby was a Soviet spy and one day we would prove it even to them.

For Philby's instant reaction to being outed by Hoover had been to appeal to his closest friend (apart from his GRU handler, Yuri Modin). This was Nicholas Elliott, who not only boosted Philby's morale by confirming that the evidence against him was flimsy but, once again, as he had four years before, played a leading role in his defence.

MI5 wondered briefly if this could be because Elliott himself had been compromised by the Soviets. The truth was more mundane and almost worse than that for, like James Angleton, Elliott was so convinced of his superior abilities that he could not for one moment imagine that he had been mistaken about his friend.

We had formed a strong mutual antipathy, as he well knew that I considered Philby to be as guilty as hell. For me, Elliott represented the worst kind of Old Etonian, full of his own importance and superior social standing. His father, Sir Claude, had been headmaster of the College. He claimed proudly that he had been recruited to the Secret Service over a glass of champagne with the head of the Foreign Office at Ascot. His influence with Menzies and rise within the service had owed something to the fact that both were members of White's, where Elliott held court at lunchtime whenever he could, amidst the country gentry and a fair number of Conservative politicians, to whom he looked to help further his career.

SIS officers were supposed to present themselves as members of the 'Foreign Service', with members of that service in turn referring to them as 'our friends'. But I heard from other members of his Club that this was not Elliott's style at all. He thought it would enhance his standing if everyone there knew that he was a spy.

My dislike of Elliott was well and truly reciprocated. Elliott was in the habit of referring to me as 'the agent of a foreign power. The representative in London of the CIA, or could it be the FBI?'

Asked to return to Washington to help to explain

Macmillan's statement about Philby to the astonished and indignant Americans, I flatly refused to do so.

Instead, I booked myself a week's holiday sailing in Bermuda with Cynthia. We called in to see Stephenson at his grand house on the island. He greeted Cynthia with hugs and kisses and complained that he had wanted to get to know her much better but had been prevented from doing so by me! I was insanely jealous about her, 'understandably so', he claimed.

She reminded him of his incognito visit to her. 'Yes, but I knew that you could see right through me straight away.'

Cynthia was thrilled to see him again. These episodes with her were never a disappointment, as we saw each other so infrequently that they were never less than passionate and, beyond that, we always felt like kindred spirits too.

A VERY BRITISH FIASCO

A year later, there followed a fiasco of a different kind, during the visit to Britain of the new Soviet leaders, Khrushchev and Bulganin, who arrived on a newly built Soviet cruiser. Naval Intelligence, on whose roster I still figured, had expressed interest in the new propulsion system of Soviet warships, but had no involvement in authorising the more than half-mad operation that followed. Any operations against the Russians during the visit in any case had been banned by the Prime Minister, Anthony Eden.

In an operation described by the Treasury chief, Sir Edward Bridges, who conducted the inquiry into it, as 'verging on criminal folly', MI6 had authorised a frogman, Lieutenant Commander 'Buster' Crabb, to conduct an overnight underwater inspection of the Russian cruiser's hull and propellers while it was docked in Portsmouth.

Crabb had a very distinguished war record as a frogman operating out of Gibraltar, but since had been semi-retired. He had become unfit, overweight and a heavy smoker with a serious drinking problem. So who on earth could have selected him for this assignment? The answer turned out to be Nicholas Elliott, who had commended him as the best frogman in Britain 'and probably the world'.

When Crabb did not return from this mission an almighty panic broke out, not only in MI6, as it was feared that he might have been killed or captured by the Russians.

When, a few days later, the Admiralty announced his disappearance during, supposedly, trials of new underwater equipment, the Russians responded by declaring that the crew had seen a frogman in the vicinity of their cruiser. Crabb had registered at his overnight hotel in Portsmouth under his real name. His MI6 handler had at least signed in as 'Smith'. The police were asked to get the page torn out of the hotel register. Crabb's body was found by some fishermen more than a year later.

Several days after Crabb's disappearance, the Russians made a formal protest, asking for an explanation about secret diving operations in the vicinity of Soviet warships in Portsmouth harbour. The Foreign Office expressed regret about the incident, while the cover-up story for a while became that Crabb had acted on his own initiative.

This was not sustainable and a furious Eden had to make a statement in Parliament declaring that what had happened had been done without the knowledge or authority of any Minister in his government.

*   *   *

Although we still had no significant agents in Moscow, a friend of mine in the British embassy, John Morgan, had managed to make inroads with their prima ballerina, Maya Plisetskaya, which he reported to the SIS station chief, as he was bound to do. Inevitably, they were followed everywhere. The feisty Plisetskaya waited until Khrushchev visited her backstage after a performance at the Bolshoi to say to him: 'My only interest in Morgan is in sleeping with him. I don't have any secrets to tell him. So please tell your goons to stop following me around!' When Plisetskaya later was allowed to dance at Covent

Garden, we tried to persuade her to defect which, unlike some other prominent Soviet artists, she firmly refused to do. She later became a friend of Robert Kennedy, who named his boat *Maya* after her.

Khrushchev, meanwhile, had rid us of the unspeakably evil former head of the KGB, Lavrentiy Beria, organiser of the Katyn massacre. In this case, instead of having to try to find out what had transpired by stealth, an official in the Soviet embassy, who doubtless was KGB, told us gleefully what had happened. One of the most senior members of the Soviet politburo, Beria had been astounded on attending what he thought would be a routine meeting to find Khrushchev making an all-out attack on him. When Beria appealed to Malenkov for help none was forthcoming, at which point Marshal Zhukov arrived and arrested Beria. This was payback for Beria's role in the wartime purge of the Red Army. Beria had been shot, we were told, wailing and pleading for his life. Among Beria's appalling features, he also had been a serial rapist of teenage girls. To our amusement, he was now posthumously accused of having been a Western agent.

*   *   *

Stewart Menzies had retired in 1952. Anthony Eden, with good reason, had been unimpressed by his successor, Major General Sinclair. I was among those who had been consulted as to who might succeed him.

'PERHAPS YOU MIGHT SEE A BIT LESS OF HER'

I was summoned by the very grand Cabinet Secretary, Sir Norman Brook, for 'a chat' in his office. I was told that I was doing extremely well, especially at getting things done, a quality sometimes in short supply in the Civil Service. He then advised me gently that I could probably not hope to become head of one of the main agencies, as I was reputed to have had an affair with one of my agents, though it might help if I saw a bit less of her.

I viewed this with some amusement, given Stewart Menzies's dalliance with one of his secretaries during the War and the peccadilloes of a friend and colleague who, later, did become head of SIS. While affairs with agents were taboo for headquarters, they had in some cases appeared to be standard operating procedure for SIS officers in the field.

I cared very little about it as, without Cynthia, I would not have been likely to have made as much progress as I had anyway. Giving her up was absolutely not an option for me. Far from seeing her less, I planned to continue doing all I could to see more of her.

The wily old mandarin, I was sure, had not missed my failure to give any undertaking from that point of view.

My recommendation, as I told Sir Norman, and that of all others outside SIS, was that Dick White should be moved across from MI5 to bring at last some more rigour and professionalism to the operations and personnel of

MI6, which over time he succeeded in doing. The change was decided before the Crabb affair and brought forward after it.

The Americans were not much interested in the Crabb imbroglio but welcomed enthusiastically the appointment of Dick White. Yet, to my surprise, Nicholas Elliott remained a senior figure in SIS, regardless of his role in the Crabb fiasco.

Before White was installed as head of MI6, a KGB colonel, Vladimir Petrov, defected to the Australians, providing a list of KGB operatives around the world. The most amusing of his revelations concerned their bungled attempt to compromise a Japanese diplomat in Canberra by taking pictures of him with two Australian prostitutes. This had misfired as when they threatened to publish the photos the Japanese had said that if they did all his friends would be proud of him.

More seriously, however, Petrov had confirmed that Burgess and Maclean had been warned by a third Soviet agent. Though confirming White's suspicions, this was dismissed by Sinclair and MI6 as being no more conclusive than the previous evidence. This led to a final interrogation of Philby, this time conducted by his friends in MI6, who concluded unanimously that he was innocent.

The MI5 representatives listening were left gritting their teeth as Philby's colleagues not only posed soft questions but suggested possible answers. When they protested afterwards, the response was that the evidence against Philby was purely circumstantial. What about MI5's own deputy head, Guy Liddell, who also had been at Cambridge and was a friend of Guy Burgess?

HOW NOT TO DECEIVE OUR CLOSEST ALLY

There followed by far the biggest crisis in our relations with the Americans since the War. While respecting his pre-War record against appeasement, the Americans had never really taken to Anthony Eden, who could be very patronising about them. Truman's Secretary of State, Dean Acheson, did not take kindly to being addressed by Eden as 'my dear'. It was not Eden's fault that neither he nor anyone else could get on with Acheson's successor, John Foster Dulles, who resented Eden's role in negotiating an agreement on Indo-China, which he held to be too favourable to the Communists. Eisenhower, who knew him from the War, had no real personal relationship with Eden either. But he did not expect to experience gross deception by him.

Eden and his Cabinet regarded Nasser's occupation of the Suez Canal zone in Egypt as posing the same kind of threat to us as Mussolini had done in the 1930s. There were exaggerated fears that the Egyptians might cut off access for our shipping to the Canal. The French government, struggling in Algeria, had similar concerns.

The Americans were playing a very different game. I

had been one of the hosts of the star CIA officer Kim Roosevelt, grandson of President Theodore Roosevelt, when he made a triumphal visit to London following the overthrow of the Mosaddegh government, which had nationalised the Anglo-Iranian oil company. Kim's role was somewhat exaggerated, as it was not within the power of the US or ourselves to generate a popular uprising in Iran, which was what had happened against the erratic leadership and economic failures of Mosaddegh. But it was Kim who had persuaded the young Shah to issue the decree dismissing Mosaddegh, as well as helping to ensure the support of the head of the Army. As this was before Eden had succeeded him as Prime Minister, we arranged for Kim to call on Churchill, who loved such tales of derring-do.

But as the leading CIA Arabist (though, unlike ours, he did not speak the language), Kim had encouraged the young officers' revolt in Egypt, led by Nasser. The US did not want to be aligned with the colonial powers. They wanted to see if they could befriend Arab nationalists. Kim's colleague, Miles Copeland, became a confidant of Nasser.

As Eden looked for a way to show his strength in responding to Nasser's seizure of the Canal, the Israelis approached him and the French with the ultra-secret plan that was finalised in a meeting at Sèvres near Paris. This was that they should launch an invasion of Egypt, providing a pretext for us and the French to intervene militarily to bring the Canal back under international control.

When the Israelis did so, British and French paratroopers then landed in Egypt and, without much difficulty, re-captured virtually all of the Canal zone only to be told, as they closed in on Port Said at the far end of it, suddenly to stop. Our military were appalled to have risked soldiers' lives only, at the last minute, to have success snatched from their grasp.

For the Chancellor of the Exchequer, Harold Macmillan, who had been the strongest supporter of intervention, had lost his nerve completely. From the very start of this adventure, there was selling of sterling on so vast a scale as to bring us close to bankruptcy without US support. But when Macmillan appealed for help to George Humphrey, his US counterpart, Humphrey flatly refused and, to Macmillan's horror, Eisenhower supported him. Having nearly regained control of the Canal, we now had to make humiliating plans to withdraw.

Eden had been trying to show that he was as strong a leader as Churchill. But, as Churchill put it, he would never have dared to invade (without the support of the Americans), 'and if I had invaded, I would never have dared to stop'. For without remaining in control of the Canal, we had no leverage to demand international supervision.

Eisenhower was hopping mad at having been deceived by Eden, who had not consulted the Americans because he feared they would oppose so risky a plan, as they certainly would have done.

Eden having withdrawn, ill and politically fatally wounded, to Jamaica, on his return he was replaced by Macmillan. In one of the major ironies of politics, the man who had contributed most, after Eden, to the disaster, was the main beneficiary from it.

But there was an important difference between the two. For Eisenhower, who could not stand Eden, really liked his former wartime colleague in North Africa, Macmillan.

This time, therefore, as I made another pilgrimage across the Atlantic to join in trying to explain ourselves to the Americans, I need not have worried, as they knew full well that the intelligence community in London had played no real part in this fiasco.

I did, however, warn them that flirting with leaders like Nasser, as Copeland and his colleagues were doing, was likely to prove of little value to them. He was trying to overthrow all pro-Western regimes and was just as opposed to American as he was to our and French influence in the region. I was glad to find that the grown-ups in the CIA agreed with me.

Meanwhile, my role in Whitehall had changed. I was now firmly based in the Cabinet Office on the Joint Intelligence Committee to help ensure continuity as the chairman always was a Foreign Office grandee with other preoccupations and more and more preparation was needed between meetings. So I was designated as a principal intelligence coordinator (which later became an official title). The purpose was to help overcome the rivalries within the intelligence community and to ensure that, when needed, a collective view was presented to Ministers, as quite frequently it had not been in the past.

I overlapped at the time with Pat (later Sir Patrick) Dean as chairman, who was hopelessly conflicted, as he had been Eden's representative in the Sèvres meeting, at which we had entered into commitments unknown to the intelligence community. Wisely, he kept a low profile for quite a while after that.

My role in the Cabinet Office earned me an invitation to a further cup of coffee with the Cabinet Secretary. Fortunately, there was no further mention of Cynthia. Instead Sir Norman again was effusively complimentary. There was just one point I might need to watch, he suggested. Perhaps I might display a bit more empathy (a word I had scarcely heard of before, and had not expected to hear from him) towards some of my colleagues.

But, leaving his office, I knew what he was referring to. For my colleagues in MI5, MI6 and Military Intelligence frequently complained to me about the deadlines and other pressures they were under, which I had to enforce. Whenever they talked to me about pressure, I would refer them to the words of my post-War sporting hero, the great Australian cricket all-rounder Keith Miller, who had been a fighter pilot during the War. Asked before a test match if he was feeling the pressure, 'a Messerschmitt up your arse, that's pressure', was Miller's response.

*   *   *

A few years later, the ghost of Kim Philby returned to haunt me once again. Following his 'acquittal' by Macmillan, Nicholas Elliott, on his own initiative, organised a job for him as a journalist in Beirut, where it was thought the wide range of Arab contacts of his father, the prominent Arabist St John Philby, could help. The proprietor of *The Observer*, David Astor, who was a confidant of MI6, agreed to pay half his salary; *The Economist* paid the other half. He also received payments from MI6. With no consultation with anyone outside his department, Elliott had managed to re-employ the man who had betrayed his entire service as an agent.

Meanwhile, I had been able to engineer a small, long-overdue and very inadequate reward for Cynthia. This had been forgotten about after the War as, despite her defunct marriage to Arthur Pack, she was regarded as American and certainly always thought of herself that way. So I asked Stephenson to recommend her and he proposed that she should be awarded a CBE. But she still clung to her US nationality and by now there was virtually no one in London who knew much about her, so that was downgraded to a grandly embossed official letter from Sir Eric Jones, the director of the Government Communications Headquarters, responsible for all our code-breaking, thanking her formally for her service during the War.

This was due to be presented by the ambassador, but I wanted the event if possible to be more special than that. As the Prime Minister was due to visit Washington, I asked his private secretary, whom I knew well, if ten minutes could be found in his programme for him to make the presentation.

So we gathered with the ambassador and a handful of Cynthia's well-dressed friends on the terrace of the embassy for Harold Macmillan to present the commendation to her. He was sufficiently intrigued by her story to invite her to tell him about it in the embassy library, with his entourage now looking nervously at their watches. He did his best to charm her and succeeded. It must have been a pleasant change for him from his wife who, despite by now being singularly unattractive, was continuing her long-standing affair with his fellow MP, the decidedly louche Bob Boothby, whom MI5 regarded as a security risk.

'SPY PLANES'

In 1959, Macmillan made the first visit to Russia by a British Prime Minister since Churchill during the War. With his usual sense of theatre, he appeared in a Russian fur hat, and at a later event, more bizarrely, in plus fours. He was hoping to defuse the tensions over Berlin and that Khrushchev was a different kind of Soviet leader, only to find that Khrushchev was different all right, but just as bellicose as his predecessors.

In May 1960, the Russians managed at last to shoot down an American U-2 photographic reconnaissance plane flying at high altitude over the Soviet Union and captured its pilot. The CIA-led programme, which had been running for the past four years, was the most important intelligence breakthrough since the War, for the U-2s were fitted with the world's first high-resolution cameras. So now at last we could see what really was going on behind the Iron Curtain, in particular so far as the Soviet Union's missiles, ships, military aircraft and heavy weaponry, including tanks and artillery, were concerned. Even if kept under cover, as the intensity of high-level surveillance increased, we could see the Soviet weaponry entering and leaving their shelters and where they were heading whenever they moved.

But when, following the U-2 incident, we explained this to Macmillan he could not have been less interested in the importance of this fundamental intelligence breakthrough, instead lamenting that what he considered the ineptitude of the Americans flying 'spy planes' over Russia would ruin the chances of his saving world peace by mediating between the US and Russians at the imminent four-power summit in Paris.

His imagined role, which appeared to be mainly for domestic consumption, was illusory anyway. Eisenhower, who attached the highest value to the programme, was contemptuous of Khrushchev's blustering about nuclear war and complaints about the US 'spy plane' when the Soviets were using all the methods of espionage they could think of against the United States. Nor was either side interested in Macmillan mediating between them. We barely managed to dissuade the Prime Minister from appearing to sympathise with the Russians at the failed summit, with Eisenhower noticing his wavering.

Ironically, when the Russians developed the same capability themselves and this was superseded by satellite surveillance, it made an important contribution to greater stability as both sides now felt that they had a clearer idea of what the other was doing.

Visiting Washington in the run-up to the 1960 Presidential election between John F. Kennedy and Richard Nixon, I found the FBI concerned about Kennedy's long string of girlfriends. Hoover, they told me, had been obliged to warn him before the War that the glamorous Scandinavian blonde he was seeing in Europe was a German agent. Now they seemed unconcerned about his affair with the actress Angie Dickinson, whom they regarded as 'classy' and were confident would be discreet, but another of his flames, who was introduced to him by Frank Sinatra, they suspected of having a connection with the mafia!

No sooner had Kennedy been elected, in April 1961, out of the blue, there followed an act of self-harm by the CIA so spectacular as to put any of ours in the shade. The Bay of Pigs fiasco cost Allen Dulles his job as CIA director, Richard Bissell being the other main casualty. As Dick White commented grimly, 'Perhaps that will stop them lecturing us quite so frequently about our traitors.'

THE TRUEST BELIEVER

It was at this time that a Polish defector identified another SIS officer, George Blake, as a Soviet spy, who proved to have been even more damaging than Philby. Blake, born George Behar in Rotterdam, had a Dutch mother and a naturalised British father who had served with us in the First World War. Blake himself served in the Dutch Resistance. He was brought to Britain by the War Office department, MI9, which specialised in retrieving members of the Resistance from occupied Europe. He became a British citizen, though he subsequently declared that he had never felt British.

He had offered his services to the Soviets while a prisoner in North Korea during the Korean War. Nicholas Elliott rehabilitated himself by helping to lure Blake back to London, supposedly to discuss a new posting.

On arrival, he was interrogated and, after a few days, he confessed. When it was suggested that he must have been coerced in captivity into spying for the other side, he replied indignantly that, not at all, he had volunteered to do so. He had worked in signals intelligence in Vienna, then spent four years with the British military government in Berlin. In that capacity, he had exposed all the SIS agents in East Germany and a high proportion of our other agents behind the Iron Curtain.

The CIA lost their first agent in Moscow from Soviet Military Intelligence, Major Pyotr Popov, who was arrested and executed. Our agents betrayed by Blake faced, as a minimum, years of forced labour; others were executed. A Dutch Calvinist who had become the truest of believers in Communism, he had as much blood on his hands as Philby.

He also had exposed, before it was even completed, the Berlin Tunnel, through which we intercepted Soviet communications around Berlin. The Soviets attached such importance to their agent that, rather than risk exposing him, they allowed the tunnel to continue operating for three years, while trying to plant disinformation through it.

So we really had it in for Blake and this complete loner had no cohort of SIS buddies anywhere around to protect him. He had done so much damage that it was decided that his trial must be held *in camera*.

The judge, Lord Parker, declared that he had betrayed 'all our agents behind the Iron Curtain' (an exaggeration, though not by all that much), forty-two of whom were believed to have been killed. He was sentenced on different counts to three sentences of fourteen years, which were to run consecutively, not concurrently; so forty-two years in total.

Witnessing Blake at his trial, I found he was by far the spy who alarmed me the most. For totally blocking from his mind the evidence of Stalin's killing of all the old Bolsheviks and his subsequent actions, here was an apparently ordinary person who believed utterly in the virtues of a totally repressive system and not just of spying but of murder on its behalf. He refused to apologise for what he had done, considering it to have been fully justified.

How was it then that we all hated Philby far more than Blake?

Though we had rescued him in the War, it was because Blake had never truly been an insider, nor truly British, not 'one of us'. While Philby had been as British as we were and of the same class. He had mingled with and befriended us with ease. He had 'fitted in', while totally deceiving us. To his former colleagues, this was his unforgivable crime.

The Americans groaned at the exposure of another very damaging agent in MI6, but at least were satisfied with the sentence. Five years later, however, came the escape of Blake from Wormwood Scrubs prison.

We had not believed that the Russians would go to any great lengths to retrieve an agent who could no longer be of any use to them, but it was not the Russians who rescued him. According to the warders, Blake had been a model prisoner and popular with some of the other inmates.

His escape was organised by three fellow prisoners, one of whom was in jail for sending a bomb to a prison officer; the other two were anti-nuclear campaigners who had broken into a US air base. They raised £200, mainly from the film producer Tony Richardson, to help get Blake out of jail. The iron struts of a jail window were sawed through and taped back into place, through which Blake escaped with a rope ladder. Abandoning his English wife and three children, he was driven all the way to East Berlin hidden in a campervan.

I could not believe that SIS and Army Intelligence between them had been so incompetent as to allow a single officer, Blake, over four years in the military government in Berlin, to know the identities or codenames of so many of our agents at the same time. As I read the riot act about this to all the agencies, measures very belatedly were put in place to ensure that no intelligence officer could ever be in such a position again. It had been a fundamental failure in our duty of care to those who were risking their lives to help us. No subsequent double agent ever again was in a position to do damage on the scale Blake had done.

Guy Burgess had died early after a miserable time in Moscow. According to the information that came our way, though he made more effort to adapt, Donald Maclean also was feeling pretty isolated there.

But not so George Blake, who was provided with or found a Russian wife. He was reported to feel entirely comfortable in Moscow, never doubting the superiority of the system there. Of all the true believers, he had proved to be the most dangerous because he was the truest one of all.

'DON'T THEY KNOW HE'S A COMMUNIST?'

In the spring of 1962, a KGB defector to the Americans, Major Anatoliy Golitsyn, was being debriefed by us in London. He identified a civil servant in the Navy department as being a Soviet spy. John Vassall had been compromised by the KGB at a homosexual party in Moscow. He was a fairly low-level spy, but he still did plenty of damage in revealing secrets about the modernisation of the Navy. In the Cabinet Office, we received concerted support from the intelligence agencies for moves in Parliament to legalise homosexuality, which was enacted in 1967. This might not have made any difference with Vassall, who was motivated primarily by money, but it did prevent others from being blackmailed in the future.

Golitsyn also was interrogated about his knowledge of the 'ring of five' agents in Britain mentioned in the Venona material and who, he specified, had met and recruited each other while at university together. All five, he confirmed, had been actively guilty of espionage.

Meanwhile, Flora Solomon, who was of Russian origin and during the Russian Revolution had been the girl-friend of the moderate leader Alexander Kerensky, by now a prominent British Zionist, had become enraged by Philby's pro-Arab and anti-Israel articles in *The Observer*. At a conference she was attending in Israel with Victor Rothschild, she recalled an attempt made by Philby to recruit her before the War and asked, 'Don't they know he's a Communist?'

Rothschild had distinguished himself working for MI5 during the War. Because he had been at Cambridge with them and had remained a friend of Philby, Burgess and Blunt, who sometimes stayed at a flat he owned in London, he came under suspicion himself for a while, though this proved to be wholly unfounded.

Flora Solomon repeated her statement to MI5, though she was not prepared to testify publicly as she feared being assassinated! Peter Wright and Arthur Martin saw using Golytsin's testimony as the long-awaited opportu-nity to make Philby pay for his crimes.

But Dick White knew the Prime Minister, Harold Macmillan, well enough to realise that this was not the extremely embarrassing outcome he was going to want. Philby, who no doubt had been warned about Golitsyn, would smell a rat if an attempt were made to lure him back to Britain and abduction was ruled out.

So White felt that he had to come up with a different plan, which horrified most of us, though we were unable to come up with a realistic alternative.

MI5, whose responsibility it should normally have been, had expected to be commissioned to re-interrogate Philby, though I doubt if that would have made any difference. When Dick White told me that the emissary was going to be Nicholas Elliott, I had no doubt what was going to happen.

Not only that, but Elliott was authorised to offer Philby immunity from prosecution in return for a full confession. The rationale that a full confession would enable us to assess how much damage he had done made little sense as, self-evidently, he had done all the damage that he could, though White was hoping to learn the identities of all his Soviet handlers. Armed with the certainty we now had from Flora Solomon, Elliott was to tell Philby that Golitsyn had been more explicit in identifying him than was in fact the case.

Even I had to feel some sympathy for Elliott's state on realising that the friend he had defended against many of us for so long was after all the traitor we had judged him to be. The sense of personal betrayal and humiliation must have been horrendous for him, though he was never likely to acknowledge this to us.

Elliott, on arrival, was greeted by Philby with the words, 'I rather thought that it might be you,' suggesting that he knew he might have been compromised. Philby was told by Elliott that his past had caught up with him. Elliott (good for him) claimed that 'we have penetrated the KGB'. As Philby continued stalling, with his usual flat denials, Elliott became infuriated, but then made the offer of immunity in return for a full confession. As Philby no doubt realised, all this was being recorded for the benefit of those of us awaiting the transcript in London.

Philby returned on the next day with a very specious document indeed. He admitted to having been a Soviet agent since 1934 and having recruited Burgess and Maclean, but claimed that he had ceased to be one from the end of the War. He had warned Burgess and Maclean, he claimed, only out of friendship. He failed to identify any of his post-War Soviet handlers.

Told by Elliott to do better if he wanted immunity, Philby produced a longer pseudo-confession and declined to identify Blunt and the Treasury official Cairncross, who were under investigation as the remaining members of the Cambridge 'ring of five'.

Philby realised that he would be subject to further interrogations until he had been 'wrung dry' and suspected that the offer of immunity could be withdrawn whenever we felt like doing so. Elliott left Beirut, handing over further debriefing to the SIS station chief there. He did so with White and others, including even MI5, delighted at his success in securing at last a confession from Philby and looking forward to extracting further admissions from him.

Worried about the American reactions, the head of MI5, Sir Roger Hollis, wrote without clearance a letter to J. Edgar Hoover, which was close to being the opposite of the truth. Hollis declared Philby's confession to be 'substantially true' and that we had no evidence of spying by him after 1946, save in warning Burgess and Maclean, so 'damage to US interests will have been confined to the period of the Second World War'.

Hoover, my friends in the Bureau told me, treated this assurance with the contempt it deserved. 'The Brits', he had contended, 'are giving us the runaround once again.'

'WE HAD NO IDEA THAT HE WOULD DO A BUNK'

Elliott was later to claim that it did not occur to him or anyone that Philby might decamp to Moscow. Yet he could not have made it easier for him to do so. Dick White did hope for more admissions from Philby but, though he did not admit it, must have realised the likely outcome. Philby was not placed under any kind of surveillance. His 'escape' from Beirut on a Soviet freighter was organised so easily that it was described as 'child's play' by his Soviet handler, Yuri Modin. Both he and Philby later came to the conclusion that his flight to Moscow was the desired outcome of Nicholas Elliott's visit.

As did I, for I had no real doubt that Dick White and, especially, the Prime Minister regarded Philby's flight as a presumably hoped-for blessing in disguise. The absolute imperative for them was not to have him facing an immensely embarrassing trial. The outcome, even after his confession, would have been uncertain as his lawyers would argue that the promise of immunity, once made, should not have been withdrawn. All other considerations were secondary to what the government saw as the overriding need to avoid a public trial.

I listened with contempt to the more braying members of SIS, who had defended Philby to the end, now saying that they would shoot him if they ever got the chance to do so, secure in the knowledge that they wouldn't.

This left us with a problem with the Americans. The CIA were furious not to have been consulted about Elliott's mission and at the sloppy outcome. White made his excuses, but I was then asked to fly to Washington once again to try to help to damp down their reactions. On my way across the Atlantic, I kept repeating to myself, 'Do not mention the Bay of Pigs!'

Like it or not, I had to start with Bill Harvey, by now close to retirement, who was feeling personally aggrieved at our failure to really try to make Philby pay for his crimes. We were, he declared, guilty of letting him, quite literally, get away with murder. He was as indignant as Hoover at the Hollis letter. 'How do you expect us to believe the rubbish that he wasn't spying during his time in Washington? What about the Albanian operation?' he enquired.

The only redeeming feature he could see in what had happened was that it had made a fool of James Angleton.

The FBI's views were unprintable about our namby-pamby way of dealing with traitors, especially as they were also following the case, about to break, of Anthony Blunt. It was a New York socialite and publisher, Michael Straight, who, very belatedly, had denounced Blunt for having recruited him while at Cambridge as a Soviet agent. Blunt did not appear otherwise to have been active since the War, but had been heavily involved in helping Maclean and Burgess to escape.

They suspected that, in this case too, Blunt would be offered immunity in return for a confession and they were right. The fact that the affair was hushed up and Sir Anthony Blunt was allowed to continue as Surveyor of the Queen's Pictures annoyed them even more. (It was not until Margaret Thatcher became Prime Minister that Blunt was exposed publicly and stripped of his knighthood.)

'YOU DON'T MESS WITH DICK HELMS'

My main target on this visit, however, was the man I believed was likely to become the next director of the CIA. This was Richard Helms, who had served with distinction in the OSS during the War. In that very East Coast patrician organisation, Helms had been the odd man out, having started as a journalist in the Midwest. I had found him to be the opposite of his freewheeling, gung-ho colleagues Frank Wisner and Richard Bissell. He had strongly opposed Bissell's disastrous venture in the Bay of Pigs. Yet he was a tough-as-nails anti-Communist, a man of few words, with natural laconic authority and an English second wife.

To all my meetings on this occasion I took with me copies of George Orwell's novels, *Animal Farm* and *1984*. Helms had read them, but most of the others had not. I pointed out that throughout the War and for a good many years thereafter we and the Americans between us had not a single agent in Moscow. In the 1930s, choosing to ignore the Stalin purges, a legion of young Americans had been persuaded to believe in Communist doctrine and the virtues of the Soviet system.

But nearly all the true believers had been recruited decades before. The boot was now on the other foot. For we were winning the most important war of all, which was the battle of ideas. There was no longer a lack of Soviet defectors and there would be many more to come. There would still be black sheep on our side, but they would be motivated mainly by money and should be easier to weed out. This was a battle we could hardly fail to win.

Helms fully embraced this doctrine and on his visits to London I heard him, with a smile in my direction, expounding on it himself. Bill Harvey had heard it from me before and it appeared to mollify the FBI.

As Helms and I both knew, it had already been validated by the case of the Soviet Military Intelligence Colonel Oleg Penkovsky, who had provided us with a vast amount of material on Soviet weapons systems and now supplied us with invaluable intelligence during the Cuban Missile Crisis. His reports (and the U-2 flights) had strengthened Kennedy's hand by revealing that Soviet nuclear capabilities were weaker and smaller than had been believed and that Khrushchev, who specialised in nuclear threats, was blustering. His contact in Moscow had been the MI6 agent and businessman Greville Wynne and all his intelligence had been shared with the CIA. On a visit to London, Penkovsky had insisted on being treated as if he were now an officer in the British Army and being dressed up in a British Colonel's uniform.

Following the crisis, Penkovsky was exposed, possibly by a US double agent, and executed. Wynne was exchanged for a Soviet KGB officer, Gordon Lonsdale, born Konon Molody, who had stolen the identity of a Canadian businessman and had organised a spy ring at our underwater weapons establishment at Portland.

Philby's disappearance, unfortunately, did not put an end to the damage he could do. For James Angleton, who was head of the counter-intelligence division of the CIA, always had been an unpleasantly driven individual. To cover his own mistakes, he destroyed all the records of his numerous meetings with Philby. The cause he adopted now, to compensate for having been personally betrayed by his closest friend, was a paranoid conviction that a whole raft of his colleagues and other Americans must be traitors too. His doctrine was that all intelligence services must be assumed to be penetrated.

The Soviet defector Golitsyn convinced him that there was a Soviet mole at the very heart of the CIA; also that he must distrust all other Soviet defectors apart from him. A *bona fide* Soviet defector called Yuri Nosenko was persecuted as a double agent. Angleton launched a whole programme of unauthorised mail and telephone interceptions of opponents of the Vietnam War. He suspected at one point that Henry Kissinger might be a Communist agent.

I was relieved to find the FBI convinced that Angleton had taken leave of his senses, leading Hoover to cut off cooperation with CIA counter-intelligence. Helms was not willing to tolerate the paralysis he caused and sidelined him, though it took far longer than it should have done before he was finally retired.

When the Watergate scandal erupted, President Nixon's closest aides, Haldeman and Ehrlichman, suggested enlisting CIA help for the cover-up.

Even Nixon blanched at this. 'You don't mess with Dick Helms,' he declared, on tape.

My meetings continued with Helms, not only in his office but often over drinks at his home in Chevy Chase, with his wife, who, by some strange coincidence, was called Cynthia!

PARANOIA IN MI5

At home, to my alarm, something similar was taking place to what was happening in the US. Used to worrying about the freewheeling style of senior SIS operatives, I now found myself more concerned about a tight-knit group of officers within MI5, led by Peter Wright and Arthur Martin. They too saw spies everywhere, suspecting Victor Rothschild because of his personal associations with Burgess and Blunt.

They had started with suspicions about Guy Liddell, who was close to the top of their own organisation, on the grounds that he too had been an associate of the Cambridge spies and had recruited Blunt as his deputy during the War. Liddell had been a friend of Blunt and Burgess. But having witnessed him, during Philby's interrogation, concluding that Philby probably was a spy, I did not believe that Liddell was one too. No proof was ever offered that he was but, having been overlooked to be head of MI5, he decided to resign, only to be offered a post with the Atomic Energy Authority, whose security clearance he passed.

With no credible evidence, they next persuaded Sir Roger Hollis, Director General of MI5, to authorise an investigation into his deputy, Graham Mitchell. Hollis felt obliged to inform the Americans about this. The CIA and FBI both contacted me to say that they had worked with Mitchell on many cases against Soviet agents, none of which had been compromised.

Undeterred by this fiasco, Wright decided to aim higher and to go after Hollis himself. Hollis was unpopular with his colleagues as he was regarded as a bureaucrat more interested in procedure than in rooting out spies, which did not make him one himself. Nevertheless, he was subjected to a freelance investigation by Peter Wright, who, as head of counter-intelligence, considered that he had a right to investigate anyone, including his boss. Hollis could not understand, he told me plaintively, what on earth he was suspected of. The Russians, we learned later, were equally mystified by the suspicions about Hollis, with whom they had no connections at all.

Wright's next suspicion was even more dramatic. Hugh Gaitskell, the impressive head of the Labour Party, died suddenly in 1963. I had known him as having an affair with Ian Fleming's wife, Ann (formerly Rothermere), while Ian fraternised with a much nicer lady in Jamaica. Wright claimed that he and a group of others in MI5 believed that Gaitskell had been poisoned by the Russians so that Harold Wilson could take over as leader of the party. Wilson had made several visits to Russia as President of the Board of Trade and Wright suspected that he must be a Russian agent, a theory also espoused by James Angleton.

In this case too there was no evidence, which did not prevent Wright persisting in his suspicions, which he shared with the journalist Chapman Pincher. One of Wilson's associates, the lawyer Lord Goodman, warned me when Wilson was Prime Minister that he was convinced that he was being bugged by MI5. I told Goodman that the only recording device in No. 10 was in the Cabinet room, in case Cabinet meetings needed recording, though the device was never used. For no Prime Minister wanted to have a blow-by-blow record of Cabinet meetings. They all preferred to rely on the records produced by the Cabinet Secretary – Sir Burke Trend, later Sir John Hunt – whose conclusions always were what the Prime Minister wanted them to be!

In reality, the only MI5 officer who believed the suspicions about Wilson was Peter Wright himself, who in due course was ousted as being 'quite mad and certainly dangerous', but not before doing more damage than he should have been allowed to do.

The British press, meanwhile, were enjoying the Macmillan government's discomfiture in the Profumo affair. Capturing the spirit of the times, it was Philip Larkin who declared that sex 'began in 1963 (which was rather late for me)'. Asked to look into this, my conclusion, to the disappointment of Wilson's creepy and conspiratorial intelligence adviser, George Wigg, was that there were no national security implications at all. John Profumo, Minister of War, had a brief fling with a young prostitute, Christine Keeler, one of whose clients was the Soviet attaché Ivanov. She also had two West Indian small-time gangster clients, who had attracted the attention of the police by attacking one another. Profumo paid the price for lying to Parliament. No secrets were disclosed by him to anyone.

But the affair made Macmillan seem as if he belonged to a bygone era. His contribution to an historic agreement by all the nuclear powers banning nuclear tests in the atmosphere did not save him from a devastating attack by one of his own MPs, Nigel Birch, quoting the words of Robert Browning: 'Never glad confident morning again!'

As the Cabinet Office had its own passage and doorway through to 10 Downing Street, I found myself being summoned there from time to time on intelligence matters, occasionally by successive Prime Ministers, more often by their private secretaries.

Next in line came Harold Wilson. A formidable domestic politician, unlike Macmillan, he did not really aspire to play much of a role in world affairs. In the intelligence community, our main role was to encourage him in resisting incessant attempts at bullying by Lyndon Johnson to get us involved in the Vietnam War which, good for him, Wilson firmly declined to do.

When Ted Heath took over, we faced a problem of a different kind. For he wanted a review of the intelligence relationship with the United States, because he feared it could complicate his efforts to be seen within the European Economic Community, which he was bent on joining, as a 'good European'. Henry Kissinger was alarmed about this and so were we, as we gained more from the pooling of resources than the Americans did. We had to brief the Foreign Secretary, Sir Alec Douglas-Home, to explain to Heath that the sharing of signals intelligence had extended since the War not just to the US but also to Canada, Australia and New Zealand in an intelligence alliance known as the 'Five Eyes' and was integral to our relationships with them. So it was decided to leave well alone.

'A VERY INTERESTING FRENCHMAN'

Cynthia had been responsible for my first and greatest coups in the world of intelligence. She was now to give a further important boost to my career.

Unsurprisingly, she had been feeling increasingly isolated in the Pyrenees, while Charles was reluctant to venture any further afield than Perpignan. Periodically, she made forays to Paris for shopping and suggested that rather than meeting in the US, an even better idea might be to meet her there. Charles, she claimed, was resigned to the fact that if he wanted her to stay with him, she had to be allowed periodic bursts of freedom.

Charles had known about me since the hijacking of the Vichy naval codes. She had told him how closely we had worked together. The War had created a strong bond between us and she needed to see me from time to time. He did not need to worry about any consequences for their marriage; there wouldn't be any. But it was no use trying to keep her like a caged animal in the Pyrenees. Charles knew her well enough to know that if he said no, she would do what she wanted to anyway. So a blind eye was turned to her not very frequent visits to Paris for shopping.

She had found us the perfect place to stay, in a suite on the top floor of the small and beautiful Hotel de Scandinavia in the Rue de Tournon on the Left Bank, just down the road from the French Senate. On sunny mornings we had our breakfast on the terrace amidst the rooftops, or walked down to the cafes in Saint-Germain-des-Prés. François Mitterrand, not yet President, could be found holding court with attractive young ladies at the Brasserie Lipp, several of whom later were appointed to posts in his administration. Drinks were often at the Rhumerie, which served heart-warming rum punches in winter, following which we would migrate to the small nightclub of Jean Castel in the Rue Princesse, a favourite of many in the French movie industry.

On the ground floor, the 'canteen' served simple bistro meals. Above it was the restaurant with benches covered in red velours and in the basement a small but well-frequented dance floor. Among the regulars were Mireille Darc, the girlfriend of Alain Delon (though Delon never appeared), the yachtsman Éric Tabarly and Marcello Mastroianni. It was impossible not to admire Mastroianni's technique on the dance floor, which was to occupy a place right in the middle and stand there glued to an attractive blonde (in fact, Catherine Deneuve), almost motionless, while the rest of us rotated around them.

*   *   *

Thanks to Charles, who knew him slightly from the War, Cynthia had been introduced, she said, to a very interesting Frenchman. This was Count Alexandre de Marenches, a prominent and very grand French businessman, who was reputed to be a friend of de Gaulle's Prime Minister, Georges Pompidou. He had grilled her about her own experiences during the War, about which he seemed to know a good deal, presumably from Charles. Would I like to meet him?

So we invited the Count and his wife to dinner at La Tour d'Argent, with its fabulous view of Notre-Dame lit up at night. The restaurant was reputed for its duck and for the fact that its famous chef had run off for a year with Ava Gardner.

The Count appeared, but not his wife, who rarely strayed from their estates in Normandy. He clearly was fond of Cynthia, who was looking at her elegant best, and she was as enthusiastic about him. I could see why, as there was no better company to be found in Paris.

The flamboyant Count had an imposing presence, as he was 6ft 4in. tall and a great *bon viveur*. His nickname was 'Porthos' after the largest and best-fed of Alexandre Dumas's three musketeers. I could see him growing ever more enthusiastic about Cynthia. When, later, he made advances to her, she politely rejected them even though, as I observed, becoming the girlfriend of the potential future head of French intelligence would well and truly have completed her CV. Thank goodness Stephenson had not been there to encourage her, I added.

'Don't get upset,' she told me, laughing.

It was a very French affair. While you were in London, we had a nice lunch at Lasserre. At the end, he asked me very politely if I would like to have an affair with him. I told him, equally politely, that in my youth I would have jumped at the chance. But now I had a husband and a lover already. I didn't want to upset you or Charles. He said that he feared that I might be offended and think less of him if he didn't at least try!

'I have had plenty of practice. This happens all the time with Charles's friends in the Pyrenees,' she added.

Alexandre was a fervent anti-Communist and loved political gossip. His particular scorn was reserved for the fellow travellers in the French intelligentsia. He described Jean-Paul Sartre to us as a 'complete little shit' who in America after the War had pretended to have been a pillar of the Resistance, whereas in fact he had never lifted

a finger against the German occupation. Unlike Albert Camus, who had risked his neck to publish the magazine *Combat* against the Germans.

Sartre, we were told, liked teenage girls, who were procured for him by his one-time mistress, Simone de Beauvoir. Camus was a far better writer than Sartre 'and a hundred times better human being'.

Nearly a third of the French still voted for the Communist Party. Eurocommunism was rubbish, they were Soviet lackeys, but at least they were in the open. What worried the Count, as it did us in London, was the prevalence of Communist sympathisers in the upper reaches of the Civil Service, including the Quai d'Orsay, which, he claimed, had its fair share of fellow travellers. The same applied, in his view, to the French intelligence agency, the Service de Documentation Extérieure et de Contre-Espionnage (SDECE).

We had ceased to share sensitive secrets with the French, as there had been leaks to the Soviets which could only have come from their Ministry of Defence. Marenches agreed that part of the problem was the quite narrow crossover between de Gaulle's anti-Americanism and the pro-Soviet sentiments of the fellow travellers.

He was immune to the fashionable French resentment of the Anglo-Saxons, his mother having been American. 'I sometimes think that they will never forgive you and the Americans for liberating us,' he observed, despite the majority having contributed little to the outcome. 'Those active in the Resistance were a fraction of the population, a few per cent of exceptionally brave men and women with the odds stacked against them, until the Germans withdrew, 'at which point we discovered that everyone had been a *resistant*'. Alexandre had served on the staff of General Juin in Italy, then France, and regaled us with possibly exaggerated tales of being present at Juin's meetings with the other Allied war leaders.

For lunches, his preferred venue was the oldest restaurant in Paris, the superb Le Grand Véfour in the Palais-Royal. It was here, when we were finishing lunch one day, that Georges Pompidou came down from one of the private rooms upstairs. The warmth of the greeting he gave Marenches left no doubt that they were indeed on the best of terms. I was introduced as 'a good friend' from England.

Our time increasingly was spent discussing Pompidou's plans. Marenches confirmed how infuriated Pompidou had been by de Gaulle's disappearance without forewarning him for two days at the height of the May 1968 insurrection. It was Pompidou who had insisted, on de Gaulle's return, on calling a general election.

This was because Pompidou, although he had made his fortune as a Rothschilds banker, had not lost touch with his roots in unfashionable Auvergne. His parents had been rural school teachers there and he prided himself on understanding '*La France Profonde*'. The Parisian leftists and anarchists trying to seize power had no support in the provinces, as the elections had shown, with massive support for the government.

But Pompidou's reward was to be dismissed as Prime Minister by de Gaulle, who feared that he was becoming too popular. To general amazement, he was replaced by the former Foreign Minister, a rigid diplomat, Maurice Couve de Murville who, according to Marenches, was 'born with a poker up his arse' and had no popular support at all.

De Gaulle's other favourite, still in the government as Foreign Minister, was Michel Debré. His one big idea, declared Marenches, amidst gales of laughter, was that the French must breed as fast as they could to catch up with the Germans. French families were being given hefty subsidies to produce more children!

By now, I was being invited, when in Paris, also to some meetings in Marenches's office on the Avenue Montaigne. In one of these I was given a message he clearly wanted me to pass on to my colleagues in London. This was that while most Gaullists were happy to see the General at loggerheads with the US and Britain, Pompidou was not one of them. He was not anti-American and still less was he anti-British. Marenches regarded this as an aberration by de Gaulle, as we would see when his friend became President, a prospect he invariably referred to as 'when', not 'if'. And as de Gaulle's aura was fading fast, it looked increasingly likely that he would be proved right.

THE PLOT AGAINST CLAUDE POMPIDOU

Over another lunch, Marenches wanted to talk about Pompidou's family. I should understand that his friend, unlike many others in French politics, was devoted to his tall, elegant and good-looking wife, Claude. She was interested in fashion, modern art and philanthropy, and he was intensely proud of her. When he was Prime Minister, he had refused to move into the official residence, the Hôtel Matignon. Instead they had remained in their flat on the Île Saint-Louis, so as to be able to spend more time together. Pompidou was immune to political attacks on him, but not to calumnies about his wife. If I wanted to know more about this, I should meet him in his office on the following day.

When I duly appeared in the Avenue Montaigne the next day, Marenches began by assuring me that his office had been swept for bugs and there would be no recording of our conversation.

He then told me a well-nigh incredible story of unscrupulousness, deception and dirty tricks, which turned out in all essentials to be true. Pompidou, as Prime Minister, had earned the enmity of the French overseas intelligence agency, the SDECE, by sanctioning its operatives for arranging the highly publicised daylight kidnapping in central Paris of the Moroccan opposition leader, Ben Barka, who was then handed over to and executed by the Moroccans.

The Pompidous knew Alain Delon and his wife Nathalie. They had met them three or four times, in the company of others; and that was all. One of Delon's bodyguards, Stevan Marković, a small-time Serbian gangster, had been murdered. His body was discovered on a rubbish dump, sewn into a mattress. He probably had been blackmailing someone, having tried to sell pictures of sex parties to the newspapers. There were also rumours of an affair with Nathalie Delon. Delon and, especially, his other bodyguard, Marcantoni, had been questioned by the police about what had happened to Marković, but no arrests were made.

Sexually explicit photographs, purporting to be of Claude Pompidou, then were found in Marković's car. In Marenches's view, some of 'those vipers in the SDECE' had been involved in planting these. Making his own enquiries, Marenches had discovered that a former police inspector, Lucien Aimé-Blanc, with links to the SDECE, had hired a 45-year-old blonde prostitute to try to look like Claude Pompidou engaging in sex with another woman.

The purpose was obvious. This was an attempt by hardline supporters of the fading de Gaulle to discredit his most likely successor. And, much worse than that, the General had done nothing to put a stop to this smear campaign and had refused to issue any expression of support for the Pompidous. Pompidou was incandescent with fury about this. Marenches doubted if he would ever speak to the General again. As for the SDECE, when he became President, they would be dealt with accordingly.

Marenches agreed that I should inform Dick White privately of this extraordinary story and of Pompidou's intentions vis-à-vis the SDECE. I also shared it with Dick Helms, who asked if Marenches was the real thing. I said that I was convinced he was and that we could expect much better cooperation from the French when Pompidou took over. I added that Marenches would be glad to meet him, but it would have to be in Paris and he would not deal with the CIA station there. So Helms set off with his wife Cynthia on a trip to France.

De Gaulle's departure came more quickly than we had anticipated. Showing how remote he had become from the new political reality, he proposed a referendum on amendments to the French Constitution, increasing the powers of the regions and making complicated changes to the composition and powers of the Senate.

You needed to be a lawyer to make much sense, if any, of this. Amidst the general inertia, to try to get it through, de Gaulle declared that if it were defeated, he would resign.

Pompidou refused to support the measure, as did de Gaulle's Finance Minister, Valéry Giscard d'Estaing, and Pompidou's availability as his likely successor was reassuring to many who, otherwise, would have felt obliged to vote for de Gaulle. So the vote was lost and de Gaulle forthwith resigned. He died little more than a year later, confirming Marenches's conviction that his health and powers had been fading for some time.

The ensuing Presidential election was won easily by Pompidou, with nearly 60 per cent of the vote. Marenches was told that Pompidou would love to have had him in the new Cabinet, but the most urgent task was to transform the SDECE. His appointment as the head of it was greeted with enthusiasm in London and by Helms in Washington.

Marenches had told me how unfortunate it was that the intelligence services in France did not enjoy the kind of prestige enjoyed by the Secret Service in Britain. The KGB was an elite service in Russia. But no one from the *grandes écoles* wanted to join the intelligence services in Paris. They didn't think it was 'in' to work for the SDECE. He needed to recruit people of a different class.

I warned him that it was because they were thought to be of the 'right class' that we had ended up with Philby, Maclean, Burgess and Blunt.

The tough-minded head of the Foreign Office at this time, Sir Denis, later Lord Greenhill, was a very unusual diplomat. He won a scholarship to Oxford and had a career as a railwayman before he worked his way up in the War to become a Colonel in the Royal Engineers, earning a military OBE.

Greenhill was infuriated by the French press publicising Philby's specious and self-serving memoir *My Silent War*, in which he had boasted how easily he had bamboozled his colleagues in SIS, while praising to the skies the skill and extraordinary human qualities of his Soviet controllers, without mentioning that the first three of them had disappeared in Stalin's purges. Declaring, unkindly, that 'the French are more familiar with treachery than we are', Greenhill had planted on Harold Evans of the *Sunday Times*, who in turn passed it to *Life* magazine, the story of how concerned we were about the prevalence of pro-Soviet elements in the French hierarchy, encouraged by the increasingly strident anti-Americanism of de Gaulle. Sir Denis added that the bestselling spy novel *Topaz* by Leon Uris, a former French intelligence agent himself, 'was based on fact', which to a considerable degree it was. For a main contributor to it had been a friend of Marenches, Philippe Thyraud de Vosjoli, head of the SDECE in the United States.

So I was asked to assure Marenches that we now looked forward to a new era of cooperation with French intelligence.

PURGE OF THE FRENCH INTELLIGENCE AGENCY

Marenches relished his new role, telling his friends in Paris society who asked if they were on the *table d'écoutes* that 'You're not important enough!' But he showed that he meant business by firing forthwith two SDECE grandees, Henri Capitant and Louis Wallon, whom he held responsible for the plot against Claude Pompidou. Those down the line who had helped them had to make their exit too.

To root out pro-Soviet moles in the French system, Marenches resorted to methods that would have been illegal in Britain. He formed a tiny, very secret unit which reported only to him. Their task was to approach suspected Communists or fellow travellers with the offer of well-paid cooperation with a friendly socialist country. Some of them were invited to Prague, where elaborate cover arrangements were made. Obviously, many did not take the bait, but Marenches rubbed his hands at the success this had achieved with a few prime suspects. The penalty, he explained, was not a trial. Instead, they were required to give up the positions they had abused and were kept under surveillance thereafter.

This brought him into direct conflict with the rival agency, the Direction de la Surveillance du Territoire (DST), which had the responsibility for counter-intelligence within France, though they could do little about Marenches's forays onto their territory so long as Pompidou was President.

105 SOVIET SPIES

By this time, having reached the Civil Service retirement age, I had to stand down from the Joint Intelligence Committee. But as the new head of SIS, Sir John Rennie, had only a rather remote relationship with Richard Helms and none at all with Marenches, I was asked to stay on for a while as an adviser to him as director of SIS.

Our main preoccupation at this time was with the proliferation of KGB and GRU agents in the Soviet embassy in London. Harold Wilson, though not pro-Soviet, did not want a confrontation with them. After Ted Heath took over as Prime Minister in 1970, his Foreign Secretary, Sir Alec Douglas-Home, wrote two letters to his Soviet counterpart Andrei Gromyko protesting about Soviet espionage activities in the UK, to no avail. When Sir Alec raised this in a meeting with him, Gromyko (who, in the flesh, reminded us of Buster Keaton) told his usual bare-faced lies. The normally imperturbable Sir Alec was flushed with anger after this encounter.

At this point, we had a stroke of good fortune. An intelligence officer in the Soviet embassy had been subject to disciplinary action and threatened with a return to Moscow because of his fondness for London nightlife. Instead, he collected his files, walked out of the embassy and drove with them to Scotland Yard. They included the names of all the intelligence agents operating from the embassy. The Russians had proved just as careless as we had been at times about the need-to-know.

There was a debate about what to do with this treasure trove. SIS were concerned about any action that would rebound against their personnel in Moscow. But the normally more conciliatory Foreign Office had a tough head of the Soviet department. He, MI5 and the rest of us saw this as the golden opportunity to expel all 105 Soviet spies, out of the hugely inflated 550-strong embassy. If the Russians expelled the same number from our much smaller presence in Moscow, it would effectively close our embassy there, in which case we would close theirs, which they would want to avoid. So the indignant Sir Alec had the pleasure of telling the Soviet chargé d'affaires that the ninety spies currently in London had to leave forthwith, and the fifteen who weren't would never be allowed to return. The Russians had to content themselves with the expulsion of 20 per cent of our 100 or so personnel in Moscow.

I had to listen to some lamentations from my SIS colleagues that we had compromised the careers of their star Russian speakers who had been expelled, but we had well and truly won this round in the battle with our adversaries. Slowly, the number of agents in the embassy and other Soviet operations in London, including Aeroflot, crept back up, but never to the levels that had triggered this action by us.

Marenches was suitably impressed by this performance, as was Richard Helms.

John Rennie, who was a Foreign Office mandarin, had become the head of SIS because it still was felt best to have an outsider in charge of the more adventurous of its officers. He had been chosen in part because he had supervised the Information Research Department (IRD) of the Foreign Office, which was a very different task. The department had been founded by Ernest Bevin and Christopher Mayhew, strongly anti-Communist members of the post-War Labour government, to counter the deluge of pro-Soviet propaganda. Its denizens included Robert Conquest, who was to write the definitive study of Stalin's terror. George Orwell contributed a list of those he knew or suspected to be covert Communists or fellow travellers. This included the name of Tom Driberg, later chairman of the Labour Party. He was by no means the only MP to be a Soviet agent. The former Labour Postmaster General, John Stonehouse, who, later, faked his own death in an attempt to disappear, was an agent of the Czech intelligence services as, we believed, was the publisher Robert Maxwell, who was of Czech origin. In 1961 the strongly anti-Communist general secretary of the Labour Party, Morgan Phillips, gave MI5 a list of sixteen 'lost sheep' – MPs whom the party leadership regarded as being pro-Soviet or Communists.

IRD joined with the CIA to help to finance the quite left-wing mainly literary magazine *Encounter*, to promote an alternative vision of left-wing politics to that of the Communists. The editor was Stephen Spender, who resigned years later when the CIA connection was revealed. This was a pity, as *Encounter* was an excellent magazine with first-class contributors, Cyril Connolly among them. None of us could see that it had ever done any harm.

Rennie, however, was not cut out to be the head of an

intelligence agency. When I arranged a lunch in Paris with Marenches, Alexandre's verdict, as I had feared, was that Sir John was 'just a diplomat', though he liked him personally. His tenure at MI6 was cut short when, sadly, his son was charged with importing heroin from Hong Kong. Rennie, being a man of honour, felt obliged to resign.

A TRUE PROFESSIONAL

So I spent the last two years of my by now part-time service in intelligence overlapping with Maurice Oldfield as the new 'C'. This was an absolute pleasure since, as Marenches observed, he was 'a true professional'. The Americans trusted him as he had acquitted himself well when serving in Washington as the successor to Philby.

Of quite modest origins, the son of a farmer, he was born in Derbyshire and graduated in medieval history from the University of Manchester. An unfailingly polite workaholic, he had served in the Intelligence Corps in the Middle East during the War before joining SIS. I knew him well from his period as the head of counter-intelligence under Dick White.

Midway through his term as head of SIS, the Irish Republican Army attempted to assassinate him with a bomb planted close to his flat in Marsham Court, Westminster, which was discovered by the security police before it went off. He was completely unruffled by this and authorised an SIS officer, Michael Oakley, to seek to open a secret channel of communication with the IRA.

Bookish and bespectacled, he compensated for an apparently solitary and lonely life by staying in his office late on most evenings and dining at his Club. He could not have been less like the buccaneers who earlier had populated the service. An excellent head of SIS, it was after I had left and he had retired as 'C' and become an adviser on Northern Ireland to a new Prime Minister, Margaret Thatcher, that he was found to have been using the services of male prostitutes. A sad discovery and his security clearance had to be withdrawn though, as Thatcher confirmed, there was no evidence that this had led to any actual breach of national security.

MADAME CLAUDE AND THE COST OF DOING BUSINESS IN AFRICA

By this time, Alexandre de Marenches was becoming very grand. As Pompidou's envoy he had become used to missions to the King of Morocco and the Shah of Iran. He had established close relations with the Israeli intelligence services, which he admired, as well as with the Saudis and the pro-Western rulers in the Gulf.

Alexandre's colleague and rival Jacques Foccart, a

holdover from de Gaulle, had made sure that the leaders of the former French colonies in Africa all had a French 'adviser' attached to their offices and were well looked after whenever they came to France, as most of them frequently did. This did, he admitted to me, entail from time to time using the services of Madame Claude, the famous French *madame* who ran a very high-class establishment indeed. Many of her young ladies, as Alexandre observed, had re-surfaced as movie stars or as the (usually) second wives of well-known Parisians. As for bribery, he contended, that was part of the cost of doing business in Africa.

This caused distress to some of my colleagues and es-pecially to the Americans, who complained to me about French 'neo-colonialism' and the fact that they could not make any headway in French-speaking Africa at all.

I asked why they wanted to. No British interests were in-volved. We had enough on our hands with our own former colonies. Those of the French, except for Algeria, had limit-ed resources. The Americans too were not really interested. We should leave most of these countries to the French.

Alexandre disapproved of Foccart, as several of the ad-visers he had implanted were after personal gain and were prone to employing dubious security personnel known as *barbouzes*, immortalised in French cinema as a cross between small-time gangsters and the Keystone Cops. He also had to reckon with the French state-owned oil companies adopting similar tactics. Marenches concen-trated on doing everything he could to thwart attempted inroads by Gaddafi and the Libyans in the Sahara region, which his friends in the Foreign Legion were successful in doing.

Despite his by now grand connections, Alexandre and I still caught up regularly when I was in Paris. I arranged a meeting with my former colleague Airey Neave, intelligence adviser to the new Leader of the Opposition, Margaret Thatcher. Alexandre had heard all about Neave, as a distinguished fellow soldier and the first successful escapee from the Colditz fortress in Germany.

Marenches had developed a love–hate relationship with James Bond. He asked me about Ian Fleming and his role in helping to persuade the Americans in the War at last to set up a central intelligence operation. As for Bond, along with the French press, in public he was disparaging about this new British hero, pointing out his hopelessness as a 'secret' agent. But, in private, he loved the films and would sneak off to see them in Geneva, or in London with me.

At one of our lunches I was told the gruesome story of General Oufkir, the sinister strong man of the Moroccan regime. Tired of having forever to play second fiddle to King Hassan, he had persuaded two Moroccan Air Force pilots to get rid of the King by shooting down his plane. They duly strafed the plane, which they were supposed to be escorting, but then were persuaded by its crew to stop firing, as the King, they claimed, had been killed.

The plane landed with the King still very much alive.

Oufkir was summoned to the palace and shot, Marenches believed, by the King himself, as summarily as Oufkir had dealt with Ben Barka.

The General had asked to meet Alexandre not long before his attempted coup. As Oufkir was banned in France, they had lunch in London, at Simpson's in the Strand, at which Oufkir had spent his time complaining about the King.

So Alexandre, who was a confidant of his, had to hasten to Morocco to assure the King that he had nothing to do with the plot. They were on sufficiently friendly terms for him to claim to me that he had told the King that, if he had been, it would have succeeded.

The French hastened to show their support for the regime, with Alexandre, as usual thinking ahead, volunteering to find advisers to help with the education of the King's son, Mohammed, including trying to mentor him on avoiding some of the excesses of his father.

Emulating Alexandre, though we could not offer the services of Madame Claude, we had established our own close private liaison with President Kenyatta and his successor in Kenya and attempted to do so with some other African Presidents as well as leaders of the liberation movements in southern Africa.

Alexandre remained head of the SDECE for eleven years. But when Pompidou was succeeded as President by Giscard, he lost his main protector. We warned him that his rivals in the DST were hatching a plot to get rid of him by accusing him of complicity in drug dealing by an SDECE agent in the US. The usual sort of articles were planted in the usual journals. This mini coup did not succeed, but Alexandre had a far more distant relationship with Giscard and was not amused, he told me, by his new master's monarchical airs. The more so, he pointed out, as the family were not really aristocratic at all. Giscard's father had been a collaborationist, though his son had joined the French Army in the last months of the War. His grandfather had simply added the appendage d'Estaing to enhance the family name.

Their relations worsened when a crisis in the hopelessly impoverished Central African Republic caused Alexandre to put an end to the reign of terror and corruption by the 'Emperor' Bokassa, who in reality was an army sergeant who had seized power. Giscard liked to go hunting there and had received a gift of diamonds from the 'Emperor', which had attracted a very hostile press. In fact, the country produced only black industrial diamonds which were close to worthless. Giscard had wanted this hushed up and felt that the publicity about the overthrow of Bokassa had made things worse.

What really upset Marenches was that his President did not want to listen to his gloomy forecasts about Soviet intentions, excluding him from the preparations for a meeting with Brezhnev in Poland, at which they merely schmoozed – a few months *after* the Soviet invasion of Afghanistan.

When François Mitterrand won the French Presidential election against Giscard, he was committed to an alliance in government with the Communists, causing Alexandre to resign forthwith. Mitterrand promised that they would not have much influence, but there was no way that our friend was going to coexist with them.

He was amused to be told by his former subordinates in the SDECE that Mitterrand had insisted on the glamorous actress Carole Bouquet having her phone tapped, but as her conversations were rarely about anything but shopping, she had been saddled with the codename 'Bird Brain'.

Alexandre was horrified when, a few years later, SDECE agents blew up the Greenpeace vessel *Rainbow Warrior* in a New Zealand port, there to protest against French nuclear tests, killing a crew member. It showed, he told me in his and my retirement, that his purge of the SDECE had not gone nearly far enough.

The Americans had fallen in love with Marenches. They felt able to talk to him in a way they could not do with any other French dignitary, and to get some very direct replies. So I heard, to my amusement, that they were planning to recruit Alexandre to be an adviser to their new President Ronald Reagan, who had met and liked him. So Alexandre continued in a new incarnation in which he was consulted on all matters to do with France, though not, he told me, on much else, while resuming his business career.

AN OWN GOAL BY MARKUS WOLF

Our worries about Western vulnerability to Soviet spying had long since switched to Germany, which was proving far leakier to the Soviets than France had been. I had no special contacts there, so this was a problem for others to deal with. Markus Wolf, deputy head (not head) of the *Stasi* for over thirty years, was a formidable adversary, though only in West Germany. The arrest of several secretaries in Bonn revealed the *Stasi* tactic of targeting overworked, relatively underpaid and often lonely personal assistants from other parts of Germany, rather than their masters.

This fairly obvious tactic, once exposed, caught the imagination of the West German press, causing Wolf to achieve cult status. He claimed at one point to have 4,000 agents in West Germany, many of them in not very significant positions. But there was evidence of successful penetration of the German contingent in NATO.

Yet it was hard to feel the same reverence for him as that shown in some sections of the press. For the primary task of the *Stasi* was to suppress dissent in East Germany, in which respect it was conspicuously failing. They had by this time had become the largest employer in East Germany, a state in which nearly everyone was supposed to spy on everyone else. Wolf was well aware that, given the chance, more than half the population would migrate to the West and thanks also to a particularly dislikeable leader, his friend Walter Ulbricht, himself a former spy, the system was failing abysmally. Beria, before his execution, had been giving his colleagues extremely pessimistic forecasts about East Germany. More than 1.5 million Germans had voted with their feet before the Berlin Wall had to be built to stop the exodus. A West German agent in East Berlin reported that on the one occasion, during a food demonstration, that Wolf had been caught up in a hostile crowd, he had been shaking visibly before being bundled off by his security detail. However skilful a spymaster, he could not overcome the reality that he was working for a failed state, devoid of any popular support.

The *Stasi* ended up scoring a spectacular own goal by bringing down the West German Chancellor, Willy Brandt, the head of whose office, Günter Guillaume, turned out to be a spy. Brandt himself was staunchly anti-Communist, as he had proved as Mayor of Berlin, but had been trying to improve relations with the Soviet Union and its satellites through his Ostpolitik. We were not worried about Willy Brandt, who remained a good ally of the US, though we were about his adviser Egon Bahr. In 1972, the Soviet Union was delighted when Brandt recognised East Germany, which previous West German governments had refused to do. The KGB, we learned (in fact, they told us themselves), were furious when the Guillaume affair resulted in Brandt being replaced by the much tougher Helmut Schmidt, who was to be a thorn in the flesh of the Russians for the next eight years. They made their feelings very clear to Wolf, who was said to be feeling 'some regret' about this outcome.

'A BADGE OF HONOUR'

Meanwhile, my friend Richard Helms had moved on from the CIA. Given his close relationship with the Shah, he was appointed by President Nixon to be the US ambassador to Iran. But his experiences over the next few years were to give us a foretaste of the new world around us in the domain of espionage. For Helms was called back to Washington no fewer than sixteen times to testify to Congress about the past activities of the CIA. This meant that he was faced with a clear conflict between the oath he had sworn to protect national security and Congressional demands that he must tell them all he knew.

Briefings to selected members of Congress on sensitive security issues hitherto generally had been able to remain confidential. From the moment the circle was widened, they frequently appeared in the press. Leaks from the information divulged to Congress led to the identification and murder of the CIA head of station in Athens, Richard Welch.

Helms was interrogated about CIA support for the Chilean opposition in the period leading to the bloody overthrow of the government of Salvador Allende by General Pinochet. Helms had told me privately that the

CIA earlier had indeed supported the opposition to the Allende government, which was full of Communists. Helms accepted that Allende was not a Communist, but his government was dominated by them and their economic policies had brought the country to a standstill.

Helms told me, and, since he had never lied to us, I believed him, that the CIA had not been involved or consulted about the coup by the Chilean military, in which Allende committed suicide and hundreds of Communists were rounded up and shot. In the hearings on his appointment to Iran, Helms had followed CIA practice in refusing to confirm support for the Chilean opposition. On the grounds that 'he had not fully and completely' testified to Congress, which he admitted, he was convicted by Congress of perjury and given a two-year suspended sentence, plus a fine of $2,000. His defence counsel said that he would wear the conviction 'as a badge of honour'. Virtually all his former colleagues supported him and raised an instant collection to pay the fine.

His successor, William Colby, concerned to avoid the same fate as Helms, adopted the opposite strategy, sharing with Congress several hundred pages about CIA covert operations, which immediately were leaked, including spying on Americans through illegal wire taps (the prerogative, when properly authorised, of the FBI) and revealing a raft of half-baked schemes, such as the idea of assassinating Fidel Castro with an exploding conch shell or cigar. Helms was contemptuous, as none of these would have had any chance of being approved by him. President Gerald Ford replaced Colby with the future President George H. W. Bush.

Under President Jimmy Carter, the head of the CIA was the very political 'reformist' Admiral Stansfield Turner. In the so-called 'Halloween massacre', he shattered morale and provoked huge resentment by reducing the CIA's admittedly inflated numbers by 800 personnel, including some very competent analysts and operators and respected senior figures. If the Agency was in need of reform, this was not the best way to go about it. There followed intelligence failures in Iran (though we did not do any better ourselves) and, much less forgivably, about Soviet intentions in Afghanistan.

By the time Ronald Reagan took over as President, the anti-CIA campaign, led by Senator Frank Church, had run its course. Helms was given a 'returning hero's welcome' at a ceremony attended by a host of senior government officials and CIA colleagues in the Grand Ballroom of the Washington Hilton, getting a standing ovation when he said that his reasons for doing what he did 'cannot be a mystery to any of you'.

Meanwhile, Helms was confiding in me about his experiences in Iran. When he had arrived, the Shah still had seemed to be firmly in control. The US had an array of listening posts on the Iranian border with Russia. The Shah, however, was suffering from the prostate cancer which eventually killed him. His illness was a major factor in his downfall, for this was in a country in which all decisions came from the top. The dismissal of his long-standing Prime Minister Hoveyda was a fatal sign of weakness. The secret police were intensely unpopular and the surge in oil prices had led to a vast amount of corruption. The Shah's modernisation programme mobilised the religious leaders against him and, increasingly, they had the support of the rural masses and the urban poor.

Helms had left before the crisis came, but his British counterpart, Sir Anthony Parsons, was there throughout. On his return, he told me that, towards the end, he had to explain to the Shah that to be able to drive through the streets to get to his palace to see him, he had to place a notice in the windscreen of his car that said, 'Death to the Shah!', a revelation that had encouraged the Shah to leave while he still could.

Helms was scathing about the Carter administration's refusal to offer the Shah, who had been a key ally for twenty-five years, sanctuary and medical treatment in the US, for fear of antagonising the new regime. Instead, he was shunted off to Panama, ending up in Egypt as the guest of President Sadat. What sort of an example did that show other US allies? And what on earth had the French been thinking of in allowing the Ayatollah Khomeini to use Paris as the platform for his rabidly Islamist propaganda? Did they really imagine that the jihadists would not turn against them?

I told Helms that Marenches had advised several times

that Khomeini should be kicked out of France, but had been overruled by his political masters, who had argued with the Shah that it was better to have him in France than back in Syria or Iraq.

Marenches himself had been obliged to do something he did not enjoy. For when the Shah found refuge briefly in Morocco, his presence there had triggered demonstrations against the monarchy. The French government and the King of Morocco had deputed Marenches to tell the Shah that he would have to leave.

THE ROAD TO KABUL

By 1980, the Soviets had become well and truly enmeshed in their war in Afghanistan and so, to a limited extent, were we.

I had driven in a jeep to and from Kabul following a liaison visit to Delhi, so I had some idea what they were up against. The mountains were vertiginous. The villages were all on peaks, not in the valleys, the better to defend themselves. The rural population were all armed. In Peshawar, on the Pakistan side of the border, you could buy in the bazaar any weapon you wanted to.

As I drove through Jalalabad, on the Afghan side of the Khyber Pass, I thought of Dr William Brydon, who, in 1842, had appeared outside the gates of our fort there, wounded and with the Afghans in hot pursuit, as one of the few survivors of our tiny army, consisting mainly of

Indian sepoys, which had been massacred in and on the way back from Kabul. Our best General, Frederick 'Bobs' Roberts, later victor in the Boer War, had become Lord Roberts of Kandahar by leading a punitive expedition which razed to the ground Kandahar and Kabul, following which, very sensibly, he decided to withdraw.

Kabul, when I visited, was still at peace and infested by Western hippies living in a haze of marijuana. In a clothes shop where I was buying a fur hat to ward off the cold, an Afghan woman entered in full *chador*, which she then took off to reveal a miniskirt beneath.

The Russians had started in 1978 by helping their Communist allies in Kabul to seize power in a bloody coup. But Hafizullah Amin then seized power within the new regime by killing its more pro-Soviet leader Taraki. This caused Brezhnev to send the Soviet Army into Afghanistan in December 1979, killing Amin and installing a Soviet stooge, Babrak Karmal, in power in Kabul.

The Carter administration, initially, had paid little attention to the goings-on in Kabul, but Carter now felt personally betrayed by Brezhnev, and his strongly anti-Soviet National Security Advisor, 'Zbig' Brzezinski, of Polish descent, was insistent that, in response, sanctions were not enough.

The CIA fell into a close alliance with the Pakistan Inter-Service Intelligence agency (ISI) and started developing a programme, which we were urged to join, to provide military support to the *mujahedin* who, under the flag of Islam, forthwith took up arms against the Soviets. From the bowels of the CIA in Langley, there emerged their Afghan experts to run this programme, coordinated by the CIA regional head, Michael Vickers. SIS had a small, segregated group to liaise with them. But as what the *mujahedin* wanted was weapons, especially handheld anti-aircraft rockets, this quickly changed into a predominantly SAS operation, ferrying weapons across the border and training the *mujahedin* to use them, which the SAS proved very effective at.

I was only involved in the early days of our operation in support of the rapidly increasing and vastly larger US effort, co-funded by the Saudis. It clearly was going to make the Soviets pay a heavier price for their invasion of Afghanistan. But I was dismayed to find that we had to ally with President Zia of Pakistan, who had been responsible for the judicial murder of former President Bhutto. Bhutto was as corrupt as most other politicians in Pakistan, but I had met and liked his daughter Benazir, in exile in Oxford.

Above all, we had reasons thoroughly to distrust the ISI, who had organised some terrorist attacks in India and whose whole strategy was to support their own proxies, the Hekmatyar clan, who straddled the border, but did little of the fighting in Afghanistan. We made sure that the SAS instead were aligned with Massoud and his forces, who were doing most of the fighting in the Panjshir Valley and the north. I also wondered if the *mujahedin* would have much interest in cooperating with us if they ever did succeed in dislodging the Russians.

Given the SAS involvement, I enforced extremely rigorously the need-to-know rules. Knowing them well, I got it agreed that they must resist their natural tendency to join in a firefight or two themselves. The head of the SAS agreed with me and, generally speaking, this rule was observed, though when I visited their headquarters in Hereford, they confessed cheerfully that they had been involved in one or two 'scrapes'.

* * *

When I visited Washington before the 1980 Presidential election, I was assured by Stansfield Turner's entourage and by his head of operations that, despite his international misadventures, Carter was ahead and sure to win. Just four weeks later, Ronald Reagan won in a landslide, revealing the 'inside the Beltway' mentality that had taken hold in Langley.

But when the pendulum swings in Washington, it often swings too far. For Turner now was succeeded by the old OSS warhorse Bill Casey, who seemed well past his sell-by date. In the words of one of my friends in the Agency, Casey 'had never seen a covert operation he didn't like'. As I still had more informants within the CIA than others, I was asked to join a meeting with the heads of our agencies to discuss how to deal with this new problem.

'So what do your "moles" in the Agency recommend?' I was asked. They were saying, I reported, that Casey was not capable of running the Agency and didn't seem interested in trying to do so. The great majority of its personnel were engaged in intelligence gathering and analysis and Casey wasn't interested in either of those. He intended to spend his time talking to the head of operations, who in turn was saying that Casey was only really interested in Afghanistan and countering and if possible overthrowing the pro-Castro regime in Nicaragua, which was trying to export its revolution to El Salvador.

My opinion was that we had no interests in Central America and should stay out of it, except in one respect. For, a year before, I had been asked to join a meeting in New York with representatives of the Guatemalan military. Their generals had appeared in uniform, looking like B-movie villains as they wore dark reflecting glasses to hide their eyes.

Our tiny colony of Belize was due to become independent and they had been threatening to invade it. If they tried to do so, we said, they could expect extremely violent retribution from the RAF. The Prime Minister had asked us to give this message to them and we could assure them that she meant it.

On dealings with the CIA, I reported that this was a

problem that was about to be solved. For an old friend from US Naval Intelligence, Admiral Bobby Inman, had already become director of the National Security Agency, the much larger US counterpart of our Government Communications Headquarters. Given Casey's incapacity, exceptionally, Inman had agreed to step in for a while also as deputy director of the CIA. We should not fear, therefore, that we would have no effective counterpart at the head of the CIA in Langley. The obvious solution was to ignore Casey, unless he contacted us directly, which he was unlikely to do, and to steer well clear of his ventures in Central America.

Inman's appointment came as a huge relief, as his support was to prove invaluable to us in the very unexpected crisis we now faced.

'THERE IS ONE THING WORSE THAN MALE MACHISMO'

It was not, I am afraid, the Joint Intelligence Committee assessment, which was that they were bluffing, but signals intelligence that forewarned us, though by barely more than twenty-four hours, of the Argentine intention to invade the Falklands. Although by then I had been put out to pasture, I was consulted by SIS because my old friend General Vernon ('Dick') Walters was the key figure in US contacts with the Argentine military.

The General, of the same generation as me, was a legendary figure in the CIA. The son of a British father, who became a naturalised American, he was educated at Stonyhurst College in Lancashire. In the War, he had served in Military Intelligence, accompanying Truman to his meeting with the insubordinate General Douglas MacArthur. Though he never went to university, he was a superb linguist, interpreting for Eisenhower with Franco and for Nixon with de Gaulle, and becoming the preferred point man for the Americans in their dealings with the Latin American leaders.

I had sought him out many times in Washington, quite frequently with Cynthia, who was fascinated by him. A walking history book, he had an inexhaustible fund of entertaining stories. He had been involved in the Marshall Plan, present at the creation of NATO and smuggled Henry Kissinger into and out of Paris for the Vietnam peace negotiations. He and Dick Helms both had threatened to resign if pressured in any way to have the CIA help Nixon in the Watergate scandal.

He had now re-appeared as the principal adviser to the US Secretary of State, Al Haig, on the Falklands conflict. As he got off the plane with Haig for their first meeting with Thatcher, I telephoned Walters to tell him what to expect. While Haig wanted to mediate, I doubted if he was going to have much luck, for Thatcher's focus was on getting the islands back. She would settle for nothing short of the Argentinians withdrawing.

As they walked into the Cabinet room, Walters told me and others afterwards, 'She seized me by the arm and steered me round the Cabinet table. On one side she pointed out the painting of Wellington, on the other that of Nelson. I think I got the message!'

Once in Buenos Aires, Walters arranged to see General Galtieri, head of the Argentine military junta, on his own. He telephoned from Haig's plane to give me an account of the conversation. Walters told Galtieri that Thatcher was determined to get the islands back, if necessary by military means. 'That woman wouldn't dare,' was Galtieri's reply.

Walters told him that 'that woman' had just allowed some IRA prisoners on hunger strike in Belfast to starve themselves to death, without blinking. 'So I wouldn't count on that if I were you,' he said. The British would fight and the Argentinians would lose, in his opinion. The bombastic General was warned that 'there is one thing worse than male machismo, and that is female machismo'.

This part of their exchange was leaked by another member of Haig's party. It was reported by the *New York Times* as a criticism of Thatcher.

A mortified Walters rang to ask us to tell the Prime Minister that this was the reverse of the truth. It was a warning to Galtieri of what was likely to be in store.

When we sank the Argentine cruiser *General Belgrano* with a heavy loss of life, Haig exploded, claiming that this had ruined his peace plan, which the Argentine military had not accepted anyway. I telephoned Walters to say that the attack on the *Belgrano* was not a political decision. It had been decided on the unanimous advice of our naval commanders, who had told the Prime Minister at her country residence at Chequers that the Argentine cruiser presented a potential threat to our naval task force. She could not possibly have overruled them.

At the moment when our forces were about to re-capture Port Stanley, having lost ships and men along the way, Haig called on us to agree a ceasefire, to save, he said, the 'honour' of the Argentinians.

I phoned Walters in a rage. Thatcher wasn't Anthony Eden, I said. Walters said that of course we shouldn't stop, and we wouldn't. He had the opposite view to Haig. For the more soundly they were defeated, the better chance of getting rid of 'those morons' in the military government. 'Your Prime Minister' might be able to claim the credit for a return to civilian government in Argentina, he said.

I attended a celebration of the Falklands victory with Walters, who had become a favourite of Thatcher, and his colleague in Washington, Bobby Inman, who told me with grim amusement that, at one point during the conflict, Haig had tried to order them to cease intelligence sharing with the British. Their response had been that nothing beyond the normal pattern of cooperation was happening – so the sharing of intelligence carried on as before.

GRENADA

One year later, it was payback time for the US support, without which we would not have been able to recover the Falklands. Except that, to my annoyance, it wasn't.

By now I was definitely retired in Oxford. And there was no question this time of being recalled to the colours, given my dissenting views. For our allies, the Americans, had invaded the tiny Commonwealth island of Grenada without so much as a 'by your leave', producing a fine outbreak of indignation from the British press and, more surprisingly, from the Prime Minister.

The Americans had been concerned about the left-wing Prime Minister of Grenada, Maurice Bishop, inviting hundreds of Cuban 'civilians' to build a new airport there. But he had then been overthrown and murdered by an appalling group of military thugs led by General Hudson Austin. The Prime Ministers of Barbados and Dominica, fearing that they might be next, had appealed to us and the Americans for help. But when the Americans asked the Foreign Office what we intended to do, the answer was nothing. Grenada was independent; it might all be very regrettable, but that was that.

The Americans had several hundred students in Grenada, studying goodness knows what. When Reagan was consulted, he said that if he did not do something about Grenada, he might as well be Jimmy Carter. When, at the last minute, he consulted Thatcher, he found, to his surprise, that she too was in do-nothing mode about Grenada and she didn't want him to do anything either.

The Americans stormed ashore, to be greeted with immense relief as liberators by the people of Grenada, who have lived under much better governments ever since. I resumed occasional pilgrimages to the beautiful Grande Anse beach there to see so for myself.

My friends in Whitehall of course closed ranks around our, to me, absurd position. In reality, a few years before, we would have solved this problem ourselves. But since we had withdrawn our solitary frigate and given up protecting these small islands, it hardly was surprising that they should look for protection elsewhere.

Meeting Thatcher at a cocktail party some months later, I said that I had just visited Grenada. Did she not regret having opposed the US intervention? Reminding me that she was a lawyer, she said that the US had violated international law. I said that I was a lawyer too. The US had sent Navy SEALs ashore to get an invitation from the Governor to intervene, which the Foreign Office had not bothered to tell her. So our exchange ended, I thought, in a draw, which was the best you could hope for with Thatcher.

OLEG GORDIEVSKY

By this time, thanks to some good fortune, SIS had succeeded in recruiting the most important of all our agents in the Soviet system. While he was serving as the KGB chief in Denmark, the tiny Danish intelligence service had noted his unhappiness about the Soviet intervention in Czechoslovakia. Not really having the capacity to do more themselves, they suggested that we might want to take an interest in him.

It was in this manner that we first heard of the KGB Colonel Oleg Gordievsky. SIS were able to establish regular contact with him in Copenhagen.

By this point, my involvement in intelligence had entirely ceased. But my colleagues subsequently revealed what he had achieved and, as a nice gesture in my retirement, invited me to meet him and his wife, a striking Azeri lady with a mane of auburn hair. She also was a KGB agent and, his defection having put an intolerable strain on their marriage, later she returned to the Soviet Union.

Gordievsky's importance to us increased dramatically when he was appointed as the chief KGB representative in London. In the following year he provided vital intelligence in alerting us to the fact that the Soviet leadership, alarmed by Reagan's anti-Soviet rhetoric, feared that a NATO nuclear drill named 'Able Archer' could be the prelude to a nuclear attack on them. The Americans had been sceptical about this account of Soviet paranoia, but we had insisted on sending through military channels an attempt to reassure the Russians. It was as well that we had done so, as further evidence later had confirmed Gordievsky's warning.

As Prime Minister, Thatcher had been proving to be far more interested in the Soviet Union than her predecessors, holding seminars about it to which SIS experts were invited. Gordievsky, who became a favourite of hers, was instrumental in focusing her on Gorbachev as a completely different type of Soviet leader, at a time when the Americans still thought that he was more of the same.

Gordievsky had become so important to us that, although we shared with the Americans most of the intelligence he provided, we did not reveal to them his identity. Eventually they worked this out for themselves, with my colleagues believing that it had been a KGB double agent in the CIA who betrayed him. Gordievsky, initially, was believed to have been given away by the American double agent, Aldrich Ames, but SIS always had a tendency to believe, when an important agent's cover was blown, that it must have been someone else's fault and never our own. It appeared, subsequently, that Gordievsky's cover had been compromised before Ames had betrayed him.

When Gordievsky was summoned back to Moscow, SIS had a carefully prepared escape plan ready to be put into action. There followed the well-known story of Gordievsky being drugged and interrogated, helped to escape from a camp where he was under surveillance and being smuggled across the Finnish border in one of our embassy officer's cars. The KGB must still have had some doubts about his guilt for them to have been so sloppy about his detention.

I had been invited back to meet him because my colleagues saw him as the most striking validation of my theory that, henceforth, the most valuable and principled defectors would be from the Soviet Union to us, rather than the other way around.

'I CAN'T SEE YOU ANY MORE'

Not long after she had introduced me to Alexandre de Marenches and the times we had spent together in Paris, I received some devastating news from Cynthia. I had been worried about her for the past two years. She had begun to appear thinner and her face was more and more drawn. I kept asking if she was getting the right medical attention. Her husky voice was getting huskier. Her cough was getting worse and it was only after a struggle that she did eventually give up smoking, though far too late.

She had telephoned me on a crackling line from France one day to say that she had been diagnosed with throat cancer and did not think that she had long to live. Charles and her daughter were looking after her and she would not be able to see me any more.

I protested very emotionally that I desperately wanted to see her again, but she was adamant, declaring that she wanted us to remain the couple we were in happier times. I tried to ring her back to no avail and she had made clear that on no account was I to try to come to see her in the Pyrenees. Her devastating illness did not take long to kill her and, I was told, was borne with her vast reserves of courage.

Her funeral, for family only, took place in a medieval church in the Pyrenees. But a memorial service then was held for her in the church of the William and Mary College in Virginia. I never doubted that I had to go, but was worried stiff about embarrassing Charles.

When I got to the church, I waited until the last minute before sitting at the back, in the last row. But on leaving the church I had to walk past Charles and their daughter greeting all those who had come. The girl looked eerily like Cynthia, despite her much darker hair and eyes. When my turn came, Charles gave me a firm handshake. 'I'm glad that you came,' he said. 'She always told me how much she loved you,' I replied, which was the truth. 'She loved you too,' was his response.

ADIEU, CYNTHIA

We absolutely never will see her like again. This memo has been intended to provide a portrait of her I don't believe anyone else could convey, and that is why I wrote it, though it covers my professional life along the way.

Her female critics found her too attractive for her own good and immoral, or at least amoral. Her skirts were too short, her manners too flirty, she liked men too much and they liked her too much as well.

My favourite columnist, David Brinkley, and his elegant wife Susan warned me that she was 'notorious' for appearing at embassy parties in Washington throughout the War clad in glamorous outfits and being too friendly with married diplomats, whose wives all hated her. Fearing that I might be subject to her wiles, they tried to warn me against her! 'Be very careful, she's a man-eater,' was their advice, echoing that of my secretary years before. They did not know about her achievements until later, when Brinkley paid a handsome tribute to her.

But even then, the methods she had used served only to confirm many Washingtonians' suspicions. They did not regard her as 'respectable'. Another term frequently used about her was 'shameless'. Even her friends regarded her as unscrupulous, which she regarded as a compliment, given the cause she had served.

For Cynthia's response was that she had signed up to do as much damage as she could to the Germans. Respectability had nothing to do with it. It was true that she was by nature an adventuress. She loved the sheer excitement of spying and of being a *femme fatale*. The thrill would leave her positively glowing.

Yet she had principles which she would never compromise. Her success as a secret agent came not just from her looks and her intelligence but from an implacable determination to do as much damage as she could to the

Nazis, whose atrocities she was familiar with, and if necessary to stop at nothing in doing so.

While not madly in love with Charles, nevertheless she loved him, taking very seriously being his wife and doing whatever she could to support him in a remote and alien environment for her.

Quite how I fitted in is not for me to say, but she was just as determined in her way, she once told me, never to let either of us down. Nor was there ever any question for Charles, any more than there was for me, of ever giving her up. So if you find her story shocking, I am afraid that I don't.

I am not sure that she was the most important female agent of the Second World War, though one of the most important she certainly was. She never had to risk her life, as Christine Granville and Virginia Hall did. Nor would she begin to compare herself, for instance, to Marie-Madeleine Fourcade, who organised a small Resistance army against the Germans (as well as executing an informer). But that was a very different role.

Yet William Stephenson described her as the 'greatest unsung heroine of the War' because, whatever may be thought of her methods, few could match her achievements.

Montgomery Hyde, my former BSC colleague in New York, wrote about her long ago, under different circumstances, and not in all respects accurately. Although much of the story came from her, she found his account too vainglorious. As she told me at the time with a grin, totally absent from his account, for obvious reasons, was going to be any mention of her relationship with me. And good for her: I approved strongly at the time. But she deserves, I feel, to be remembered as she really was – and I would like her not to be forgotten now.

ENVOI

There was a chapter my friend and mentor didn't write, so I interrogated him about it. This was to reflect on what lessons he had learned from forty years' experience of working in the world of secrets.

These were, he said, of course the difference extraordinary individuals can make, starting with Cynthia and his friend Stephenson, with Dulles, Helms and Walters in the CIA, Penkovsky, Gordievsky and others who had risked their lives to help us. The Russians no doubt would say the same of their atom spies, of Richard Sorge in Japan and of Blake and Philby.

Next, the negatives, for we must never fail to understand that by their very nature, secret agents are capable of deceiving anyone, including themselves. In how many cases, he asked, did we find that an agent was working for more than one master; or was embellishing or cobbling together their reports from snippets in the local press; or whose prized sources or contacts were simply invented by them?

For espionage always had attracted some of the very best, but many more of the worst, with all shades of grey in between.

Intelligence from human agents frequently proved unreliable, as many were willing to mislead for purposes of their own. It was a certainty that we ourselves had employed far more double agents than we ever imagined and even now we did not realise who all of them had been.

'That is why,' he added with a smile, 'I have never been surprised that so many of our secret agents, from Compton Mackenzie through Graham Greene to John le Carré, have proved to be such excellent writers of fiction!'

The other most frequent failure, he contended, was in assessing the intentions of our adversaries on the basis that they were like us, only on the other side.

More often than not, they were not like us at all. Yet we assumed that they would act 'rationally' from *our* perspective, even when there was no reason to believe that they would do so. The Joint Intelligence Committee assessment on the eve of the Falklands War was that the Argentine generals would not invade; they were merely huffing and puffing.

We had been dealing with 'rational' adversaries in the IRA, in that they always tried to get away. But there were just as many 'irrational' adversaries, who were prepared to perish with their victims.

In dealing with other intelligence agencies, as he had spent a lifetime doing, we had to ask ourselves who we could really trust. The answer could never be provided by the title, but only by the character and our direct knowledge of whoever we were talking to.

We had to proceed on James Angleton's grim assumption that every intelligence service had been penetrated. This was why he had spent three decades in the unglamorous and never-ending task of improving vetting and enforcing the need-to-know.

He had encountered heads of the CIA he would have entrusted with his life, and others (probably meaning Stansfield Turner) he did not trust at all.

No doubt they would say the same about us, the problem being also not whether they told us the truth, but how much of it, for few of our counterparts were able to tell it all; and nor at times were we. So the question to be asked was not 'Has he/she told me everything?' but 'Have they ever misled me?'

The future of espionage, he declared, depended now more than ever on technology.

Aerial surveillance was worth 10,000 spies and was far less likely to mislead us.

Our opponents had to communicate; otherwise they could achieve little against us.

So signals intelligence would remain as vital as it was in the Second World War. For although, these days, our enemies all knew that their communications would be attacked and interception could be made ever more difficult through encryption, no adversary had yet proved able to defy the efforts of our cryptographers using super-fast computers over an extended period of time. Non-state actors could not do so at all.

The Middle East remained the epicentre of explosive religious antagonisms, not only between Israel and the Arabs but between Shia and Sunni Muslims too. In terms of fanatical and irrational actors, it was the most unstable area of the world. If a nuclear weapon were ever used again, that is where it would most likely be.

The nature of warfare was undergoing the same revolution. The decisive advantage in future conflicts would go to those most proficient in electronic warfare, ranging from self-guiding missiles, the blinding of the adversary's communications and infantrymen who would be robots.

'I am glad that I am not going to be part of this,' he concluded. 'Spying was a lot more fun with Cynthia.'

*　　*　　*

I have been glad to help to edit this document and thanks are due to James Stephens and James Lilford, and to Biteback for publishing it in recognition of the extraordinary role played by Elizabeth Thorpe, codenamed Cynthia, in helping the Allied cause in the Second World War and the light it throws on our dealings with the US and French intelligence services thereafter.